THE
CIVIL RIGHTS
MOVEMENT

STRIVING FOR JUSTICE

REFORM MOVEMENTS IN AMERICAN HISTORY

The Abolitionist Movement

The Civil Rights Movement

The Environmental Movement

The Ethnic and Group Identity Movements

The Family Values Movement

The Labor Movement

The Progressive Movement

The Women's Rights Movement

REFORM MOVEMENTS
IN AMERICAN
HISTORY

THE
CIVIL RIGHTS
MOVEMENT

STRIVING FOR JUSTICE

Tim McNeese

CHELSEA HOUSE
PUBLISHERS
An imprint of Infobase Publishing

Cover: Civil rights advocates gather at a school athletic field in Tallahassee, Florida, prior to a demonstration in March 1964.

The Civil Rights Movement: Striving for Justice

Copyright © 2008 by Infobase Publishing

Chelsea House
An imprint of Infobase Publishing
132 West 31st Street
New York NY 10001

Library of Congress Cataloging-in-Publication Data
McNeese, Tim.
 The Civil rights movement : striving for justice / Tim McNeese.
  p. cm. — (Reform movements in American history)
 Includes bibliographical references and index.
 ISBN-13: 978-0-7910-9504-1 (hardcover)
 ISBN-10: 0-7910-9504-5 (hardcover)
 1. Civil rights movements—United States—History—Juvenile literature.
 2. African Americans—Civil rights—History—Juvenile literature. 3. United
States—Race relations—Juvenile literature. I. Title. II. Series.

 E185.61.M4794 2007
 323.0973—dc22

                              2007021717

Chelsea House books are available at special discounts when purchased in bulk quantities for businesses, associations, institutions, or sales promotions. Please call our Special Sales Department in New York at (212) 967-8800 or (800) 322-8755.

You can find Chelsea House on the World Wide Web at http://www.chelseahouse.com

Series design by Kerry Casey
Cover design by Ben Peterson

Printed in the United States of America

Bang EJB 10 9 8 7 6 5 4 3 2 1

This book is printed on acid-free paper.

All links and Web addresses were checked and verified to be correct at the time of publication. Because of the dynamic nature of the Web, some addresses and links may have changed since publication and may no longer be valid.

0783

CONTENTS

1

A Defining Moment

From the base of the Washington Monument stretching west along the still reflecting pool to the marble steps rising up to the Lincoln Memorial, a great sea of humanity waited with excitement, holding its collective breath in anticipation of America's future. On that hot summer day, August 28, 1963, those who could reach the reflecting pool's edges dipped their feet into it to cool themselves. The gathered crowd could be heard from blocks away as people conversed with their friends, shouting across the way when they spotted someone they knew. They were happy to be part of something that they realized was immense in scope and as monumental in purpose as the nearby limestone obelisk, that is dedicated to America's first president, George Washington.

There was music in the air, literally, as well-known performers, especially folk singers—Joan Baez; Bob Dylan; the activist trio of Peter, Paul and Mary—and black musicians, including Odetta and Mahalia Jackson, entertained the assembled crowd. The words of Woody Guthrie, perhaps the greatest folk songwriter of the previous generation, could be heard throughout the Capitol grounds: "This land is your land, This land is my land, From California to the New York Island." Some of those assembled carried signs that expressed their desire to be treated equally: "We Demand an End to Bias NOW!" "We March for Effective Civil Rights Laws NOW!" The common theme was clear: Blacks, with support from sympathetic whites and others, were demanding what had been denied them for too long—decent treatment and equality. They did not intend to wait any longer to get it. They wanted it NOW.

A WORLD OF DIFFERENCE

In the America of 1963, life was generally better for the nation's blacks than it had been during any previous time, but comparisons between eras could never tell the real story. The fact was that, even a century after the Civil War, which began the process of freeing the South's 4 million slaves, the average black American still faced discrimination, an existence defined by poverty, misery, and racism. In 1963, unemployment among blacks in the United States was more than twice that of whites. With the country still enjoying the prosperity of the 1950s, the average white family's annual income was $6,500, but a black family could expect to earn $3,500, a little more than half of what a white family earned. At every turn, many black Americans could expect to be treated as second-class citizens, facing discrimination in school, at work, on the road, in the grocery store aisle, at the theater, in the hospital, and even in church.

During the previous decades, there had been promises of a better tomorrow for America's blacks, but the movement focused on lobbying efforts and litigation. The call for patience was always the pacifier used by many whites, most of whom did not intend to take any overt steps on behalf of black equality or an expansion of black rights. Change was always spoken of in the future tense—but the country's largest minority had become tired of waiting. They were fed up with not being treated equally and had become more proactive, ready for action and even confrontation.

"Confrontational" was the best word to describe the handful of years that led up to 1963. Some of the most intense violence of the civil rights movement had taken place during the previous six months alone. The city of Birmingham, Alabama, a Southern metropolis of 350,000, noted for being perhaps the most completely segregated city in the entire country, had experienced some of the most horrific treatment meted out to civil rights advocates during the previous decade. Blacks had finally risen up to protest their treatment by local whites. Even though blacks accounted for two of every five residents in the city, they were victims of racism. Blacks in Birmingham were three times less likely to be high school graduates than whites. Fewer than 20 percent were trained for jobs that required some specialized skill. Most black families in the city made less than $3,000, below the national average for their race. Racism was prevalent and indiscriminate throughout Birmingham, even relentless in its scope: During a 1956 performance in Birmingham, famous black singer Nat King Cole was assaulted by whites and beaten on the very stage where he had been performing. The following year, a group of drunken white men grabbed a black man randomly off the streets, drove him out of the city to a remote shack, and castrated him.

BIRMINGHAM AND "BULL"

In the spring of 1963, racist whites in Birmingham outdid even themselves. Angered by organized black protesters, city officials, led by Public Safety Commissioner Theophilus Eugene "Bull" Connor, arrested them by the hundreds. On May 2, civil rights organizers responded by sending black Birmingham children into the streets to replace them and take up the cries against racism. They marched from the 16th Street Baptist Church. Ranging from 6 to 18 years old, the schoolchildren marched for four hours, singing the freedom songs popular among civil rights advocates. Connor ordered nearly 1,000 of them arrested and hauled to jail in paddy

During the spring of 1963, Martin Luther King Jr. and other civil rights leaders organized Project C to confront segregation in Birmingham, Alabama. After the Birmingham police arrested many adult protesters, the Southern Christian Leadership Council decided to send out thousands of African-American children to protest segregation. Here, policemen round up a number of black children near Birmingham's city hall on May 4 of that year.

wagons. There had been so many of them that Connor had to use school buses to transport the overflow to jail.

Black organizers were undaunted: The following day, more than 1,000 children skipped school and gathered at the church for their march of protest. Then, Bull Connor ordered police and firefighters to unleash a fury of violence against them. These young protesters would be taught a lesson not soon forgotten. Policemen wielded their nightsticks and unleashed trained attack dogs on the black children. Firemen turned their fire hoses on the children. Streams of water sprayed out, knocking them to the ground. At 100 pounds of pressure per square inch, the fire hoses were strong enough to knock the bark off a tree. Children struck the streets and sidewalks with immense force and were slammed into parked cars. A black businessman called a city attorney from his storefront, frantically explaining to him what he was seeing: "Lawyer Vann, they've turned the fire hoses on a black girl. They're rolling that little girl right down the middle of the street."[1]

The anger welled inside the hearts and minds of Birmingham's black population. The following day, blacks hit the streets, some carrying pistols and knives. The city would not abuse their children in that way again. Civil rights leaders, including Baptist minister Reverend Martin Luther King Jr., the eloquent voice of the movement, encouraged their fellow blacks not to stoop to the level of Birmingham's officials. In the days that followed, protesters remained in the streets. By May 6, 2,000 more demonstrators had been arrested and put in jail. There were so many who were incarcerated that they were being held at the Alabama state fairgrounds.

The confrontations escalated. There were more firehose assaults, dog attacks, and police clubbings, this time against adults. Through it all, Birmingham blacks risked their very lives for their beliefs. Meanwhile, throughout the country, Americans were shocked at the images that they saw on their black-and-white televisions, violence between black protesters and white officials delivered to them between shades of gray. From the White House, President John F. Kennedy Jr. watched somewhat helplessly. He had no authority over the violence in this Southern state. Federal issues were not at stake, it seemed to him, even as Alabama governor George Wallace sent in 500 National Guardsmen. With his options limited, Kennedy had already dispatched a federal official to Birmingham in an attempt to negotiate a settlement between the two opposing sides and bring about an end to the violence. Fortunately, an agreement was reached between civil rights leaders and some of the city's leading businessmen, who agreed to the demands of Birmingham's black residents to desegregate the city's downtown business district. For the moment, the violence was brought to an end and Birmingham was no longer burning with hatred.

In the aftermath of the racial violence in Birmingham, President Kennedy took steps in support of the civil rights advocates. On June 11, Governor George Wallace made a dramatic attempt to keep blacks from enrolling in the University of Alabama, a segregated state school, by literally standing in the doorway of the university's main building. Recent court decisions had mandated the desegregation of such public institutions of higher learning. That evening, President Kennedy went before the American people on television and gave his support to a package of proposed civil rights legislation:

> The fires of frustration and discord are burning in every city. Redress is sought in the street, in demonstrations, parades and protests which create tensions and threaten violence. We face, therefore, a moral crisis as a country and as a people. . . . I am . . . asking the Congress to enact legislation giving all Americans the right to be served in facilities which are open to the public—hotels, restaurants, theatres, retail stores, and similar establishments. This seems to me to be an elementary right. Its denial is an arbitrary indignity that no American in 1963 should have to endure.[2]

The following week, Kennedy delivered his newly proposed civil rights bill to Congress. Its purpose was to eliminate a long legacy of segregation in America. It was straightforward in what it espoused: Segregation in all interstate public accommodations would be rendered a federal offense. The U.S. attorney general could file suits against schools that did not integrate, and he could also order that federal funds be denied to any state in which federal programs remained segregated. The proposed legislation also defined a potential voter as one who had a sixth-grade education, the new definition of "literate."

"PASS THE BILL"

With this legislation on the table, the various civil rights organizations leapt into action. They did not intend to allow this package of privileges and promises to be shot down by an uncooperative or unresponsive Congress. Just the previous year, Congress had done just that to another civil rights bill, one not nearly as strongly worded as the new one. King and various leaders of the movement pondered the best way in which they could make their wishes clear to the political leaders in Washington. They made their decision quickly: They would organize a massive march on the nation's capital filling the streets of Washington with as many people as they could in support of civil rights legislation.

News of the march on Washington spread quickly across the country that summer, announced and trumpeted through hundreds of local chapters of civil rights organizations, church groups, and pulpits. Modes of transportation took on special names, such as "Freedom Buses" and "Freedom Trains," delivering excited supporters of the movement that had experienced a difficult summer of disappointment and even failure. Altogether, approximately 30 special trains were chartered and 2,000 buses were filled to capacity with blacks and whites from every corner of the South and beyond, everywhere the call of civil rights had listeners. Some of the organizers of the march feared that attendance might be low, perhaps no more than a few thousand people. They worried that their important symbolic gesture might fail. By the

On June 11, 1963, President John F. Kennedy delivered his famous civil rights message to the American public in which he laid the groundwork for what would become the Civil Rights Act of 1964. Kennedy is pictured here with a group of leaders from the March on Washington. From left: Whitney Young, National Urban League; Dr. Martin Luther King, Christian Leadership Conference; John Lewis, Student Non-violent Coordinating Committee; Rabbi Joachim Prinz, American Jewish Congress; Dr. Eugene P. Donnaly, National Council of Churches; A. Philip Randolph, AFL-CIO vice president; Kennedy; Walter Reuther, United Auto Workers; Vice President Johnson; and Roy Wilkins, NAACP.

day of the march, however, the nation's capital was playing host to a teeming throng of advocates for black equality and opportunity that numbered a quarter-million strong. Nearly one of every four was white. Never in the history of the United States had such numbers gathered anywhere in

America in support of the simple cause of human rights and human dignity.

The people had gathered, black and white alike, in support of the proposed civil rights bill that would be sent to Congress. The themes of the march included unity, harmony between the races, and a banner cry of "Pass the Bill." The great gathering in Washington was planned for a single day. Organizers wanted the event to begin by 9:00 A.M. and finish before sunset. There was the street music to entertain, but the most important part of the day was centered on a series of speeches to be delivered by various civil rights leaders. With the microphones set up on the front steps of the Lincoln Memorial, the vast crowd listened as best they could to one speaker and then another. Each called for the passage of the proposed bill, but some marchers were critical that the legislation did not go far enough. Late in the day, the leader of the civil rights movement rose to deliver his address.

VOICE OF THE MOVEMENT

Martin Luther King Jr. had been a faithful servant of the movement for black equality since the mid-1950s. He had helped organize the great Montgomery bus boycott in 1955 and had been among the first to call for black protests against segregation through nonviolent means. His voice had consistently been one of religious conviction that advocated social change. Few civil rights leaders were more respected among the nation's blacks, as well as whites who were sympathetic to the movement, than Reverend King. King, however, had come to doubt the ultimate success of the movement he had championed for eight long years. There had been serious setbacks in the spring, and the highly publicized clashes in Birmingham had won only limited victories—and they had come at a great cost. In addition, success seemed to be coming about too slowly.

Despite these shortcomings, King would deliver more than just another speech in support of equality for black Americans on that August day in 1963. His speech would be a defining moment for the movement, and his words would give new measure to the cause and inspire civil rights advocates to continue their cause. He spoke with the conviction of a minister of the gospel on racial harmony and mutual respect:

> I have a dream that one day down in Alabama . . . one day right there in Alabama, little black boys and black girls will be able to join hands with little white boys and white girls as sisters and brothers. . . . With this faith we will be able to work together, to pray together, to struggle together, to go to jail together, to stand up for freedom together, knowing that we will be free one day.[3]

His words were excitedly received that afternoon in Washington—but would they bring about change? Would the weary warriors for black equality continue their struggle? Would justice prevail ultimately or would white racism continue to rule in America?

2

A Legacy of Racism

The story of American history has always included controversial issues concerning race and race relations. Among the generation of English subjects who established Jamestown, the first permanent English colony in North America, black Africans were imported against their will, first simply as workers but within a few decades as slaves. Throughout the remainder of the colonial period in America, slavery took root as Southern economies in particular came to rely on black labor in its tobacco, grain, and rice fields. By the time of the American Revolution (1775–1783), hundreds of thousands of people were being held in bondage.

SLAVES IN AMERICA

Those who fought for their own freedom from British authority during the American Revolution gave some thought to the freedom being denied the colonies' slaves. Some patriots, both Southerners and Northerners, expressed doubts about speaking out in favor of liberty and not including blacks. In the end, though, slavery remained intact. America's Founding Fathers—Thomas Jefferson, John Adams, Patrick Henry, and others—gave their support to the new nation's first cherished document, the Declaration of Independence, but they did not apply its enduring phrase "all men are created equal and endowed by their Creator with certain inalienable rights" to black slaves. Slavery would continue after the revolution, even as the colonies became states.

There were some brighter moments for slaves after the United States became a nation. Although the country's constitution, established in 1789, protected slavery in all of the states, many of the Northern states took steps to abolish the institution. In states such as New York, Pennsylvania, and those of New England, slavery had never been deeply rooted and was relatively easy to remove. There was even some expectation that slavery might die a natural death by the end of the eighteenth century or early in the nineteenth century. Tobacco prices, which had long justified the broad expansion of slavery during the 1700s, were dropping by the early 1790s. Without this important cash crop, slavery would no longer be profitable for many slaveholders.

The institution was rescued by the invention of a simple device called the cotton gin. In 1793, a Northern inventor named Eli Whitney designed a tabletop device that featured rollers, rows of nails, a containment hopper, and a hand crank that could clean the sticky green staples, or seeds, out of long-staple cotton at the rate of more than 50 pounds a day. Cotton had never been profitable in the South because of the bottleneck in production caused by the problem of seed removal. With this simple stroke of Whitney's mechanical genius, cotton became the new cash crop of the South and slavery began to flourish. Southerners quickly spread out into new lands across the Gulf Coast, from Alabama to Texas, during the years between 1800 and 1830. Cotton was the mainstay of the Southern way of life, and slave labor facilitated its producion.

Throughout the first half of the nineteenth century, the overarching issue in American politics became the expansion of slavery into the country's western territories. It became a flash point between Southern slaveholders and

Northerners who believed in the labor of free men, even if they did not believe in equality between blacks and whites. For three generations that spanned the first 50 years of the 1800s, slavery became further ingrained in Southern society. The conflict over the institution's expansion ultimately led to armed conflict between those who wanted to see slavery's expansion go on unrestricted and those who wanted to see it contained in a single region of the country. In the 1860s, the North and South went to war, at first over states' rights (the rights of the Southern states to take their slaves wherever they chose) and only later directly over whether slavery would continue to exist within the borders of the then-fractured American republic. The national conflict pitted American against American and involved 3 million men in uniform who fought on numerous battlefields in engagements that ended in the deaths of more than 600,000 blue- and gray-clad soldiers. President Abraham Lincoln, who personally opposed slavery, brought the issue to the forefront by issuing the Emancipation Proclamation on September 22, 1862. It went into effect on January 1, 1863, as the Civil War was still raging. This executive document would be the first brick in the wall against the continuation of slavery.

NEW BIRTH OF FREEDOM

The Emancipation Proclamation was only a beginning. It forbid slavery in regions of the South that were already under federal military control, but it did not end the institution. That could not be done directly by the president; it required an overt act by Congress. Two years after Lincoln's first step, the Northern-led U.S. Congress passed the Thirteenth Amendment to the Constitution during the final spring of the Civil War. (The states would ratify the amendment in December 1865, making it law.)

On September 22, 1862, President Abraham Lincoln issued the Emancipation Proclamation, which promised freedom for slaves who lived in the states of the Confederacy. Lincoln is depicted in this 1864 painting by American artist Francis Bicknell Carpenter with his cabinet during the drafting of the proclamation. Left to right: Secretary of War Edwin M. Stanton, Secretary of the Treasury Salmon P. Chase, Lincoln, Secretary of the Navy Gideon Welles, Secretary of the Interior Caleb B. Smith, Secretary of State William H. Seward, Postmaster General Montgomery Blair, and Attorney General Edward Bates.

The new amendment abolished the institution of slavery. This would be Congress's first step in radically changing the lives of millions of black slaves in America. The following year, the Republican-controlled Congress passed the Fourteenth Amendment, which was ratified in 1868. This amendment granted citizenship to all former slaves. All of this placed an ironic twist on the direction that the U.S. government had followed just a decade earlier. In 1857, the U.S. Supreme Court had decided the case of *Dred Scott v. Sandford* and determined that America's blacks, even those who were free, "had no rights that white people were bound to respect."[4] The war had changed America and the American mindset.

Further inroads against the institution of slavery and the denial of freedom to millions of blacks were made when Congress passed yet a third amendment to the Constitution. In 1869, the national legislature passed the Fifteenth Amendment, which granted the right to vote to black men. In the words of the amendment, "The rights of citizens of the United States to vote shall not be denied or abridged by the United States or by any State on account of race, color or previous condition of servitude."[5] Perhaps, at last, racial equality in America would finally take place. The new amendment appeared to be the "culmination of the crusade to end slavery and give black people the same rights as white people."[6]

BLACK CODES

The hope for change soon faced serious challenges, but this was nothing new to blacks across the South. At the end of the Civil War, white leaders across the South had met to determine the new future of their former slaves. Laws that would come to be known as Black Codes had been passed in 1865 and 1866; the purpose of such laws was to keep blacks from achieving true equality. Their rights were typically denied to them under the Black Codes: The newly freed slaves, now known as "freedmen," were kept from enjoying basic freedoms such as owning a gun, buying property, entering into contracts, testifying in a courtroom, and serving on juries. Some of the Black Codes denied blacks access to public places such as stores, steamboats, and trains. Hotels, inns, and public restrooms were often closed to them, as well. In several Southern states, including Georgia, Arkansas, and Texas, black children were not allowed to attend public schools or even to learn to read. Of course, white Southerners tried to deny the vote to former slaves.

Such blatant and obvious attempts to curb black freedoms were addressed, in part, by Congress through the passage of the Thirteenth, Fourteenth, and Fifteenth amendments. Additionally, more specific laws were soon passed to counter the measures taken by Southerners to keep blacks from their new constitutional rights. In early

TO PROTECT THEIR NEWLY WON FREEDOMS

Both during and after the American Civil War, the United States Congress took drastic and well-intended steps to not only end slavery, but also to guarantee the rights of blacks throughout the country. Although the federal government took the leadership in making attempts to alter the relationship between blacks and whites and to provide freedoms for former slaves, blacks themselves sometimes took important steps toward these same goals.

Black Codes were put in place in several Southern states during 1865 and 1866, and blacks saw these new state laws as challenges to their freedom. Throughout the South in both years, they organized and met in their own conventions to protest the restrictive codes. Many of those who led the fight were professionals, including ministers, teachers, and artisans. These conventions did not represent any significant militant or radical stance on the part of blacks but provided forums for them to figure out ways to preserve their newly won rights. The blacks who participated in such convention meetings typically called on whites to support the laws being passed to protect black rights.

Such conventions met throughout the South and took several different forms. In Raleigh, North Carolina, black delegates met in the African Methodist Episcopal Church, where they called for the recognition of their equal rights and the privilege to vote. At a Georgia convention, the appeal was, again, for equality. In

1866, Lyman Trumbull, a Northern senator from Illinois, introduced two bills to protect blacks. The first helped provide additional monies for the Freedmen's Bureau, a federal government agency officially known as the Bureau of Refugees, Freedmen, and Abandoned Lands, which was established in early 1865. The bureau was formed to "help freedmen obtain land; gain an education; negotiate labor contracts with white planters; settle legal and criminal disputes involving black and white people."[7]

a written statement, the convention called "not for a Black Man's Governor, nor a White Man's Governor, but for a People's Governor, who shall impartially protect the rights of all."[*]

In Charleston, South Carolina, blacks held two separate conventions. The first was held before the passage of Black Codes, and the second followed them. At the first convention, blacks had been conciliatory, emphasizing how they held white residents of the city with "respect and affection."[**] They even suggested that, if blacks received the vote, only those who were literate should be granted suffrage. The second convention, held after the Black Codes were in place, took on a different air. Black delegates condemned the codes and drew up a list of demands, including the rights to vote and to testify in court, access to public schools, and the opportunity to become landowners.

Such conventions clearly reflected the wants and desires, as well as the expectations, of Southern blacks, but they were typically ignored by whites. Even President Andrew Johnson's policies appeared antagonistic to blacks who sought life in a new South. One black veteran of the Union Army put his feeling into words: "If you call this Freedom, what do you call slavery?"[***]

[*] Darlene Clark Hine, *The African-American Odyssey.* Upper Saddle River, N.J.: Prentice Hall, 2005, p. 275.
[**] Ibid.
[***] Ibid., p. 276.

FIRST CIVIL RIGHTS BILL

Trumbull's second bill was nothing less than "the first civil rights bill in American history."[8] The intent of the proposal was clear: It stated that anyone born in the United States was a citizen and that his rights were guaranteed by law. (Ironically, the exception to the rule was American Indians.) To make certain that the Southern states accepted the legislation, the bill threatened to deny congressional representation to any state that made overt attempts to keep blacks from voting. The Trumbull measure would not become law without a fight. President Andrew Johnson (Lincoln had been assassinated in 1865, and Vice President Johnson became the chief executive), a Southerner by heritage, vetoed the bill, but Congress overrode his opposition and passed the Civil Rights Act of 1866. The following year, another act, designed to keep Southern states from creating artificial barriers to black suffrage, was passed. The Reconstruction Act of 1867 called for the dismantling of the postwar white-controlled state governments of the Southern states, only to replace them with rule by the federal military. Martial law was declared across the former Confederacy, and the South was divided into five military districts.

This measure was a bold step by Congress to ensure that the North could impose its will on the Southern states. The period that followed, which lasted from the end of the Civil War until 1877, was known as the Reconstruction Era. During those 12 years of federal control of Southern state politics, blacks were not only allowed to vote but also to hold political office, denying whites the exclusivity of the privilege that they had held for so long. Throughout the 1870s, hundreds of black men were elected to represent the legislatures of every Southern state that had taken up arms against the United

States during the war. Blacks were even elected to the U.S. Congress for the first time in American history. There would be black county officials, as well as sheriffs and mayors. In some Southern cities—including Little Rock, Arkansas, and Tallahassee, Florida—blacks were elected to the position of police chief. It was a new day politically for the South and for America's black population.

Yet, as these significant steps were taken by Northern white men in power who were compelled to aid Southern blacks, the strong influence of racism remained in both the North and the South. The federal government could pass all the laws it wished to promote equality, but the majority of white Americans were not yet prepared to treat black equally. Blacks were considered inferior in every way— physically, intellectually, socially, and psychologically. This deeply ingrained racism caused black equality to largely remain a matter of legality only. Such racism can be seen in the words of Benjamin F. Perry, a Johnson appointee who served as the Reconstruction governor of South Carolina: "The African has been in all ages, a savage or a slave. God created him inferior to the white man in form, color, and intellect, and no legislation or culture can make him his equal . . . it is in vain to think of elevating him to the dignity of the white man."[9]

Even in the face of strong Northern influences and control over the post–Civil War South, once the Southern states had returned to the Union and Reconstruction had come to an end, they took subversive steps to defy federal laws that were supposed to guarantee civil rights for blacks. The Fifteenth Amendment may have intended to guard black voting privileges, but Southerners created state laws to thwart that intent. In 1871, after Georgia was readmitted to the Union, the white-controlled state legislature began to require a poll tax before anyone could vote. The law kept many poor blacks who could not afford to pay the tax from voting. To make certain that no poor whites would also be denied voting privileges, additional laws called "grandfather clauses" were created. Such laws stated that, if a person could not afford to pay the poll tax, he could still vote if his grandparents had been qualified to vote. This obviously applied to the vast majority of whites. At the same time, a person could not even register to vote if one of his grandparents had been a slave.

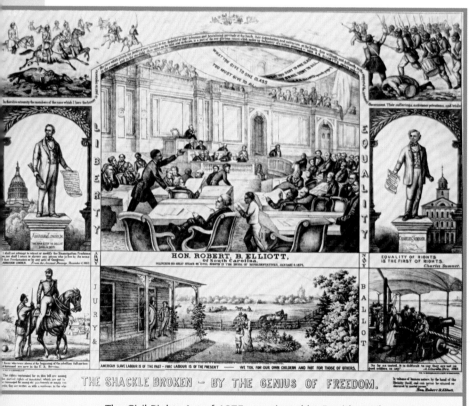

The Civil Rights Act of 1875 was signed by President Ulysses S. Grant in March of that year and guaranteed that every U.S. citizen, regardless of race, color, or previous condition of servitude, had the right to equal treatment in public places. U.S. Congressman Robert B. Elliott (R-South Carolina) is depicted here giving a speech in the House of Representatives in support of the act.

NEW LEGISLATION

With all previous legislation having failed to ultimately guarantee black rights in the South, the U.S. Congress took yet another step on behalf of America's largest minority by passing the Civil Rights Act of 1875. This act was intended to fill in the gaps that existed between the Thirteenth, Fourteenth, and Fifteenth amendments and the Civil Rights Act of 1866. The wording of the act was carefully constructed to eliminate as many loopholes as possible: "That all persons . . . shall be entitled to the full and equal enjoyment of the accommodations, advantages, facilities, and privileges of inns, public conveyances on land or water, theater, and other places of public amusement."[10] The act was well intended and contained all the best ideals that the U.S. government could represent, and it became law as the Reconstruction era was coming to an end.

After 12 years of exerting pressure on the South, the federal government had become weary of holding the South at arm's length. Many Southern states had already been readmitted to the Union, and, for many, the Civil War was but a memory. By the time the Civil Rights Act of 1875 was passed, conservative white Democrats had regained control of their state governments. Only Florida, Louisiana, Mississippi, and South Carolina remained "unredeemed," having not regained federal state status. In addition, many Northerners had lost interest in supporting the political and social rights of blacks. By 1877, Reconstruction was officially over, leaving the Southern states in control of not only their own political destinies but also of the destinies of their black populations. In short order, many of the gains made by blacks over the previous 15 years began to melt away like snow during a spring thaw.

Segregation Nation

The Civil Rights Act of 1875 caused many Americans, both black and white, to have hope that, in the decades to follow, equality would become more of a reality on the social landscape. The intent of the act was to plug the gaps in the 1866 Civil Rights Act to achieve something closer to racial equality for the country's minorities. The hope lasted only a few years. The federal government took few significant steps to enforce congressional legislation. Then, in 1883, the U.S. Supreme Court struck down the act, declaring it unconstitutional. The primary reason given by the court's majority for killing the law was that it violated the Fourteenth Amendment to the Constitution. The amendment had been created to protect blacks from racism, discrimination, and segregation established through state laws. The 1875 law could apply only to states, then, but not to any discrimination practiced by private citizens and businesses. Once again, blacks and other American minorities took another step backward in their pursuit of greater freedoms and privileges.

A COURT DECISION

Early in the 1880s, blacks found little on which to hang their hopes regarding civil rights. Reconstruction and its protections provided by the federal government had come to an end in 1877, and the Civil Rights Act of 1875 was no longer binding. To complicate matters further, Southern state governments, as well as public officials, businesses, and private citizens, moved quickly after Reconstruction to stop efforts to bring civil rights and equality to blacks. At its most extreme, this effort led some whites to join a secret organization based on terror and intimidation. White racists established Ku Klux Klan chapters throughout the South, dressing up in white costumes with hoods to disguise their true identities. The organization was not new in the 1880s, having been founded by Confederate veterans within a year of the end of the Civil War, but it expanded its membership at this time, becoming "a terrorist paramilitary force whose main function was to intimidate black citizens who attempted to register to vote or demanded other civil rights."[11] With their hoods hiding their faces, Klansmen went to great lengths to frighten blacks, employing tactics such as beatings, burning homes and belongings, and sometimes resorting to murder, killing anyone, black or white, who attempted to aid blacks in any way. Their tactics were so extreme that even many Southerners could not abide by or support the Klan.

In addition to the radicalism of the Ku Klux Klan, Southerners used a variety of other tactics to intimidate and frustrate blacks who wanted civil rights. Southern politicians thumbed their noses at national laws that were designed to provide and protect rights for blacks by passing state laws. Such state efforts were often focused on keeping blacks from gaining political power through voting. After Reconstruction, voting among blacks in the South dropped dramatically. Just a few examples provide a picture of what blacks were often up against: In 1876, around the end of Reconstruction, South Carolina was home to

Founded in 1866 by veterans of the Confederate Army, the Ku Klux Klan was organized to resist Reconstruction. In addition to intimidating carpetbaggers (Northerners who moved south during Reconstruction), the group also terrorized blacks in the South. In this drawing by Frank Bellew, which appeared in the February 24, 1872, issue of *Harper's Weekly*, a Ku Klux Klan member aims a rifle at a black family in the South.

90,000 blacks who voted in the presidential election. By 1888, because of state laws that restricted blacks' access to voting, the number had dropped to fewer than 14,000. Despite a greater than 80 percent drop in black voters in their state, South Carolinians were not satisfied. In 1895, the state legislature altered its constitution, adding an "understanding clause." Patterned after a similar law in Mississippi, this statute allowed illiterate people to vote only if they were able to understand a passage from the U.S.

Constitution when it was read to them. This allowed voting officials to be extremely subjective, often denying black interpretations while allowing nearly every white voter's interpretation of what they had heard. Such laws caught on and, by the end of the 1890s, nearly every Southern state, with the exceptions of Kentucky and West Virginia, had passed such restrictive laws on allowing blacks to vote. The federal government took almost no steps against such blatant tactics designed to push blacks out of the political process.

Additional laws poked and prodded at the gains made by blacks regarding equal rights over the previous 20 years. By the end of the nineteenth century, every state that had been a part of the Confederacy during the Civil War had created an intricate set of laws, all designed to restrict black political and social equality:

> These racist laws made blacks feel inferior because they were denied basic human rights. Even toilets and drinking fountains were marked 'White Only' and 'Colored.' . . . It was evident to black citizens that their separate places to eat, sleep, or travel were in much worse shape than those reserved for whites. But the southern whites who had regained power pretended that the separate services for blacks were equal to those of whites.[12]

In the minds of Southerners, the long-standing belief in the inherent inferiority of blacks remained an unspoken, yet widely accepted, matter of fact.

SEGREGATION BECOMES THE NORM

Many of the laws passed throughout the South during the 1880s and 1890s were based on segregation, a fundamental concept designed to keep the races from direct contact with one another. Although the racist view of black inferiority had been a tacit understanding for previous generations of Southerners, interaction between and intermingling of the races had remained commonplace. During the days of slavery, obviously, contact was required between owner and slave. Even during the generation after the Civil War, segregation had been almost unheard of in the South. (The word "segregation" was rarely used at all until the twentieth

PLESSY V. FERGUSON AND SEPARATE BUT EQUAL

"Jim Crow" laws found a new legitimacy during the 1890s, when the U.S. Supreme Court decided one of the most important race-related cases of the nineteenth century—*Plessy v. Ferguson*. Jim Crowism was applied to the nation's transportation systems just as it was to nearly every other aspect of life for America's blacks. In fact, one of the earliest segregation laws was passed to restrict blacks' access to passenger trains. The Tennessee legislature led the way in 1881, and other Southern states had jumped onboard before the end of the decade. Generally, these laws established "separate but equal" use of railcars by blacks and whites—at least in name. Railroad companies were required to maintain separate, but equal, railcars for blacks and whites to establish segregation in interstate transportation. The cars reserved for black passengers were generally not equal in quality and style to the first-class cars that were reserved for whites, though. (Second-class cars were set aside for blacks, regardless of whether they might be able to afford a first-class ticket, as well as for whites who smoked or chewed tobacco.) These segregation laws were not popular with the railroad companies, because such legislation required the companies to maintain at least twice as many cars as they might need if the races were given equal access to first-class cars.

Blacks found these Jim Crow laws insulting and degrading. They easily saw through the sham claim of "separate but equal." When Louisiana passed such a segregation law in 1891, it was immediately opposed by a black organization formed specifically to challenge the law—the American Citizens' Equal Rights Association of Louisiana. The group century.) Blacks and whites had always mixed on a social level, if unevenly. There had been few laws focused on restricting such interaction. Whites took steps to restrict blacks by enacting laws after the war, but those laws did not restrict contact. There had been a window of connectedness between blacks and whites, but by the latter decades of the

well-to-do black Louisianans, including 18 black state legislators. This early civil rights organization decided to challenge the law in 1892 using a black man from New Orleans named Homer Plessy (he was actually an "octoroon," meaning that he was one-eighth black). Despite his limited black heritage, Plessy was considered black by law, although he was so light skinned that he could pass for white. Plessy boarded a whites-only, first-class rail car in New Orleans and was arrested (the railroad cooperated with the entire arrangement). The incident was organized in the hope that his case would result in the segregation law being struck down as unconstitutional because the railcars provided for whites and blacks were separate but by no means equal.

The case wound its way through the legal system until it came before the U.S. Supreme Court. *Plessy v. Ferguson*, decided in 1896, would be a disappointment to many hopeful blacks who chaffed under segregation. In an eight-to-one decision, the highest court in the land upheld the Louisiana railroad segregation law, stating, "merely because it required separation of the races, [the law] did not deny Plessy his rights, nor did it imply that he was inferior."[*] The decision was a watershed event in the future of race relations in America for more than the next 60 years. No longer would the U.S. Constitution's Fourteenth Amendment afford blacks equal consideration and treatment under the law. "Separate but equal" would remain the law of the land.

---

[*] Darlene Clark Hine, *The African-American Odyssey.* Upper Saddle River, N.J.: Prentice Hall, 2005, p. 318.

1800s, whites took steps "in a quest to channel the relations between the races,"[13] creating laws to divide them. The result was that most Southern institutions, including schools, courthouses, hospitals, poorhouses, orphanages, and even insane asylums became segregated. Probably a majority of white-owned hotels, inns, taverns, and restaurants were off-limits to black patrons. Even churches "quickly broke into different congregations for blacks and whites."[14] Where laws and official policies did not technically make certain institutions off-limits to blacks, it was understood by many Southern blacks that they were "not [to] venture where they felt unwelcome or where they were likely to meet hostility."[15]

All of these legal and social alterations brought on results that are mirrored in the words of an 1885 Memphis newspaper editorial: "The colored people make no effort to obtrude themselves upon the whites in the public schools, their churches, their fairs, their Sunday-schools, their picnics, their social parties, hotels or banquets. They prefer their own preachers, teachers, schools, picnics, hotels and social gatherings."[16]

Southern state legislatures passed a veritable avalanche of hundreds and hundreds of restrictive segregation laws, statutes that were often referred to by a common name: "Jim Crow" Laws.

DECADES OF DISGRACE

Throughout the next two generations, as America entered the twentieth century, blacks found life restricted by law as it had not been since the days of slavery. Segregation and Jim Crowism were further institutionalized. Blacks, especially in the South, found themselves denied opportunities at every turn. It sometimes appeared that blacks had no rights, especially given the prevalence of lynching—the hanging of an accused black person by whites without the benefit of trial. The practice became common during the 1890s. Between 1889 and 1932, approximately 3,750 people were lynched in the United States, most of them in the South. Although some victims were white, the vast majority of them were black men. Such lynchings were typically practiced by members of the white middle and lower classes, and well-educated, professional whites did little to protest or condemn the practice. Those who participated in lynchings were almost never arrested or put on trial.

The fact was that, even in the early twentieth century, most white Americans still believed that blacks were inherently inferior. This idea was being challenged during the early 1900s by black professionals who would soon establish the first prominent movement in support of equal rights for their race. Leaders included Booker T. Washington and W. E. B. Du Bois. These two black leaders were contemporaries, but they did not agree on how to solve the problems under which blacks struggled. Du Bois would take a harder stance than Washington and in 1909 would be crucial in helping to establish one of the most important black civil rights organizations in the country—the National Association for the Advancement of Colored People (NAACP). His words make his goals for America's black race clear: "I believe in Liberty for all men; the space to stretch their arms and souls; the right to breathe and the right to vote, the freedom to choose their friends, enjoy the sunshine and ride on the railroads, uncursed by color; thinking, dreaming, working as they will in a kingdom of God and love."[17]

He was the civil rights leader of his time, and, with his leadership, the NAACP launched a fight that it would continue throughout the twentieth century. One of its chief campaigns was to tear down segregationist barriers. In 1915, the organization had one of its first legal victories with the U.S. Supreme Court decision *Guinn v. United States*, which overturned a grandfather clause in Oklahoma. Then, two years later, NAACP lawyers brought down another state segregation law, this time in Kentucky, which denied blacks the right to live in white-majority neighborhoods. The decision—*Buchanan v. Warley*—was another crucial win for the civil rights organization and blacks throughout the country.

These legal victories for blacks and the NAACP took place against a backdrop of continuing racism and segregation in

Founded by W. E. B. Du Bois, Ida Wells-Barnett, Henry Moscowitz, Mary White Ovington, Oswald Garrison Villard, and William English Walling in 1909, the National Association for the Advancement of Colored People (NAACP) was established to support the rights of African Americans. Here, members of the NAACP march to protest lynchings in 1917.

the United States through the years after World War I (1914–1918). Blacks had joined the U.S. military and participated in "the Great War," and they had done so despite the fact that the military was segregated, organized on the basis of Jim Crowism. Tens of thousands of blacks returned from the conflict dissatisfied with their lives, especially in the South, and chose to migrate north, taking up residence in Northern cities from Chicago to Detroit to Cleveland to New York. By the 1920s, one fact was obvious: There was a growing discontent among at least an element of the nation's black population. No longer would they accept second-class status, economic discrimination, and the constant denial of their inherent rights.

In the 1920s, the NAACP entered its third decade. The black civil rights organization had led the legal fight against segregation, and its membership had mushroomed after World War I from 9,000 members in 1916 to 10 times that number by 1920. It experienced singular success during the 1920s as it fought for antilynching legislation in Congress and against segregation in the courts.

The 1920s would also be a decade of white defiance toward blacks. The Ku Klux Klan experienced phenomenal growth as millions of white men joined its ranks, and millions of other white Americans supported them in the spirit of racism. Then, the economic nightmares of the Great Depression of the 1930s took their toll on blacks throughout the country as "the fall of the economy pushed many black Americans to the edge of starvation."[18] Some of the gains made during previous years by blacks were lost during the Great Depression.

WAR AND SEGREGATION

In the late 1930s, as World War II began to move beyond Europe, the U.S. economy was directly and dramatically affected. With the Allies, especially Great Britain and France, buying so many weapons and other war materials from U.S. manufacturers, the U.S. economy began to recover. American factories, mills, shipyards, and production plants had shifted into high gear, producing massive numbers of planes, tanks, ships, and trucks. There seemed to be work for everyone. Some blacks found new job opportunities, but many did not. Labor unions, including the American Federation of Labor (AFL), did not allow their employers to hire blacks or other minorities. Even government programs such as the U.S. Employment Service (USES) hired only whites as defense workers. Old practices of discrimination and exclusion based on race were not abandoned, and "most jobless African Americans were left waiting at the gate."[19]

By 1940, blacks came together to protest these discriminatory practices. A massive rally was organized in January 1941, led by the president of the Brotherhood of Sleeping Car Porters, A. Philip Randolph. He proposed that 10,000 blacks descend on Washington, D.C., for a great march in the nation's capital to say, "We loyal Negro-American citizens demand the right to work and fight for our country."[20] The March on Washington Movement (MOWM) drew up its demands, which included convincing the government to refuse to offer defense contracts to companies that discriminated racially, plus a call for an end to segregation in America's armed forces. (At the time, the military accepted blacks into service at the same rate that blacks represented the general population, approximately 11 percent. They would then serve in their own units in menial jobs. The Army Air Corps accepted no blacks at all.)

So many blacks responded to Randolph's call to march that the estimate of the number that might come to Washington to participate reached 50,000. The proposed march immediately drew a response from President Franklin D. Roosevelt. It concerned him that such a protest would give America's enemies ammunition to question the country's commitment to the democratic way of life. He sent his wife, Eleanor, and the mayor of New York City, Fiorello LaGuardia, to meet with Randolph and request that he cancel the march. When this failed, Roosevelt himself sat down with the Randolph. In June 1941, Roosevelt gave in to Randolph's demands and issued Executive Order 8802, which stated, "I do hereby affirm the policy of the United States that there shall be no discrimination in the employment of workers in the defense industry or government because of race, creed, color, or national origin."[21] Randolph and his supporters had succeeded in changing government policy, based only on the threat of a massive march on Washington. Although Randolph had upped his estimates for participation to 100,000 by the time he talked with President Roosevelt, it is unclear that he could have produced anywhere close to that turnout. He had bluffed the president, and Roosevelt had folded.

This presidential declaration, Executive Order 8802, represented the first significant action taken by a U.S. president against race discrimination since Lincoln had issued the Emancipation Proclamation in 1862. Excited blacks were soon disappointed when they realized how ineffective the order would prove to be: Many companies hired only a small number of "token" black workers, and labor unions still discriminated in their membership because they were not even mentioned in the president's order. Although Randolph tried to continue his fight, blacks found it difficult because many government agencies, especially the military, dragged their feet on implementing Roosevelt's order. In addition, by December 1941, after the Japanese attack against U.S. military installations in Hawaii, especially Pearl Harbor, the vast majority of the American people believed that it was more important for everyone to be loyal to the country and win the war against foreign tyranny than to take up the call to fight discrimination at home.

SERVING AS "SEPARATE BUT EQUAL"

Throughout the war, the U.S. military maintained a policy of "separate but equal," continuing to segregate blacks and other minorities in their own units. The result was that the majority of the one million black Americans who served during World War II were assigned to "auxiliary units," which were usually transportation and engineering corps. Many blacks loaded and drove trucks to the battlefronts as part of the Red Ball or White Ball Express, for example. Black soldiers built ports, bridges, roads, and camps and performed basic, nonfighting tasks.

Back in the United States, black organizations protested these demeaning and racist discriminatory policies. A. Philip Randolph took up the cause, as did the leaders of the NAACP, the National Urban League, and other secondary groups, such as the National Association of Colored Graduate Nurses. Editorials against these policies appeared in the pages of black publications such as *The Crisis* and *Opportunity*, published by the NAACP and the National Urban League, respectively. In time, given protests by these civil rights organizations, plus that of the press and even black U.S. military officers, the War Department eventually began to respond positively. Part of the problem in allowing blacks to serve alongside white troops was racism, both among the white soldiers and in the general public. The War Department cooperated with black leaders in producing a training film titled *The Negro Soldier*, directed by popular movie director Frank Capra, in 1943. It was a well intended but "patronizing film [that] emphasized the contributions black soldiers had made in the nation's wars since the American Revolution."[22]

During World War II, more than one million African Americans served in the U.S. military, but due to the military's "separate but equal" policy, most were assigned to transportation and engineering units. Here, members of a black transportation regiment prepare to be shipped overseas in December 1944.

The War and Navy departments made additional efforts to satisfy blacks and reduce the level of practiced racism. As the war dragged on, the Navy Department accepted blacks as sailors and noncommissioned officers (NCOs). By 1942, the U.S. Marines, which had always been solely white, took black recruits, and, by the following year, the U.S. Navy was accepting black Americans into officer training programs. Only the Army Air Corps failed to create integrated officer training schools. Black units were sent to fight during the remainder of the war, and "several African-American artillery, tank destroyer, antiaircraft, and combat engineer battalions fought with distinction in Europe and Asia."[23]

Such steps taken by America's white military brass went beyond those taken by their predecessors, but the level of racism during World War II remained high. The battle for racial equality was being fought, but it was unclear whether that particular conflict was being won. It must be said, however, that a new generation of black Americans who were allowed to fight on battlefields and man the guns of the nation's greatest ships at sea were gaining experiences that would forever change them. Many of them returned to their homes different than when they had put on their uniforms for the first time. They returned to civilian life "with an enhanced sense of themselves and a commitment to the fight for black equality."[24]

The black veterans of World War II were much more likely to support meaningful change against racism than those who had served during World War I. It appears that, unlike the black veterans of the earlier world conflict, many more black World War II veterans went into military service with better educations, including high school and college degrees. This better-educated generation of blacks was more likely to already hold "radical" ideas in opposition to racism generally, as well as against specific military policies such as segregated units and facilities. In one postwar sociological study of veterans who returned home to Chicago, researchers made the following observation:

> At least half of the Negro soldiers . . . were city people who had lived through a Depression in America's Black Ghettoes, and who had been exposed to unions, the Communist movement, and to the moods of racial radicalism that occasionally swept American cities. Even the rural southern Negroes were different this time—for the thirty years between the First and Second World War

has seen a great expansion of school facilities in the South and distribution of newspapers and radios.[25]

During the war, black Americans had been exposed to a whole new world. They had seen other places, had fought for their country, and had returned expecting anything but the status quo. They had fought against those who had sought to deprive entire populations from China to Poland of their basic civil rights. Now they expected their country to provide these same basic rights to them. The attitude of many returning blacks seems to have been captured in the words of a Mississippi veteran, Douglas Conner, who served with the 31st Quartermaster Battalion on the Pacific island of Okinawa. He was convinced that the service he and other blacks had made to the U.S. war effort gave them "a sense that they could succeed and compete in a world that had been saying that 'you're nothing.' . . . "Because of the war." Conner summed up, "I think many people, especially blacks, got the idea that we're going back, but we're not going back to business as usual. Somehow we're going to change this nation so that there's more equality than there is now."[26] The change was coming—but how far no one knew. The war would result not only in the defeat of fascism abroad, but would help to give rise to great changes across America's varied racial landscape.

4

The Fight in the Courts

As World War II altered the expectations of many blacks in the United States, the campaign for change was, in some circles, already underway. The NAACP had never abandoned its struggles against segregation, even in the dark days of the Great Depression. Considering the courts as one of the most viable ways of challenging segregationist laws, the NAACP had continued its march forward. In the early 1930s, the organization gained a new chief legal advocate, Charles Houston, who was then serving as the dean of Howard University Law School, a traditionally black school. Houston would spend much of his brilliant law career fighting cases on behalf of the NAACP to help strike down segregationist restrictions, especially in education. Houston would establish the first civil rights law course taught in any American law school. Using Howard as his drawing board, Houston would make his law school "one of the best repositories of legal materials and files on civil rights precedents in the country."[27] Other law schools began to consider Howard as the magnet law school in the struggle against Jim Crowism and segregation. Both Howard and the NAACP's legal wing would be greatly served by Charles Houston, and later, by one of his protégés, a young Howard Law School student named Thurgood Marshall, who graduated in 1933.

TAKING ON "SEPARATE BUT EQUAL"

During the 1930s and 1940s, Houston and other attorneys who worked for the NAACP won key cases. Houston had decided to target segregation in universities and colleges, especially graduate schools. In 1936, through one of his cases, *Pearson v. Murray*, Houston succeeded in getting the U.S. Supreme Court to declare the student acceptance program at the University of Maryland to be unconstitutional because the university accepted only white students and denied blacks entry—a clear violation of the concept of "separate but equal." Then, in 1939, after Houston decided to step out of his deanship and service to the NAACP to go into private practice with his father, Thurgood Marshall stepped into his position.

During the next 10 years, Marshall led the efforts of the Legal Defense Fund, the legal wing of the NAACP, in its fight against "separate but equal." Under his leadership, NAACP attorneys won additional cases, including *Lane v. Wilson* (1939), a Supreme Court decision to strike down another Oklahoma law that restricted black voting. Two years later, the Supreme Court decided *Mitchell v. United States*, striking down an Arkansas law that required blacks to ride on segregated railroad cars. In 1944, Marshall himself argued before the Supreme Court, winning the case *Smith v. Allwright*, which ended a Texas law that denied blacks the vote in primary elections. Then, in 1946, Marshall won another key Supreme Court decision, *Morgan v. Virginia*, which struck down a Virginia law that had denied a black woman the right to sit on the seat of her choice on an interstate bus.

Marshall and other NAACP attorneys would also be involved in important cases that related to segregation in education. In 1950, Marshall savored the sweet success of winning back to back cases before the Supreme Court.

Sweatt v. Painter and *McLaurin v. Oklahoma State Regents for Higher Education* were both concerned with blacks being denied entry to professional schools, including the University of Texas School of Law in Austin. The success of each of these cases won by the NAACP hinged on the promises of "separate but equal." With these Supreme Court decisions, the legacy of *Plessy v. Ferguson* seemed closer to an end. In 1950, Marshall's success in the courtroom prompted him to question how much longer "separate but equal" could remain intact: "The complete destruction of all enforced segregation is now in sight. . . . Segregation no longer has the stamp of legality in any public education."[28]

LIGHT AT THE END OF THE TUNNEL

Then, in 1952, Marshall appeared ready to make his prediction come true. Through a package of five separate cases, all related to black children being denied access to public schools, the U.S. Supreme Court agreed to hear them collectively as *Brown v. Board of Education of Topeka*. Although several NAACP lawyers were involved, as were attorneys not employed by the civil rights organization, Thurgood Marshall would play the key role in the case. Although the case was argued and reargued and delayed because of the death of the court's chief justice, Fred Vinson, justice would be served when the U.S. Supreme Court decided unanimously in favor of Marshall and his colleagues. *Brown v. Board of Education of Topeka* would strike a deathblow against the 60-year mandate of "separate but equal." At long last, *Plessy v. Ferguson* had been overturned. Public schools throughout the country could no longer be kept segregated.

Despite the landmark *Brown* decision of 1954, school administrators and boards throughout the country, especially in the South, dragged their heels and refused to make the

The landmark *Brown v. Board of Education of Topeka* decision overturned the "separate but equal" mandate established by *Plessy v. Ferguson* in 1896. Although the 1954 *Brown* decision made segregation illegal, many years would pass before schools were fully integrated. Here, three of the attorneys who were involved in the case—George E. C. Hayes (left), Thurgood Marshall (center), and James M. Nabrit—pose outside the U.S. Supreme Court after the historic decision.

appropriate changes to integrate their schools. In 1955, a second ruling, titled *Brown v. Board of Education II*, put schools on notice: They must integrate "with all deliberate speed."[29] Even with this legal demand by the high court, desegregation in America's schools did not take place overnight. The struggle over equal rights for blacks in the United States in 1954 seemed, in some ways, only beginning.

SEGREGATION AND THE 1950s

During the 1950s, the United States experienced a decade of greater prosperity than had existed at any other time in its history. The majority of Americans would come to own their own homes and enjoy a higher standard of living than that of previous generations. The cold war was raging between the two superpowers, the United States and the Communist-led Soviet Union, which caused a certain amount of uneasiness and uncertainty for many U.S. citizens, but still the 1950s would be a golden era in American history. This was true for the vast majority of whites, but not for the majority of the nation's blacks.

In many respects, the beginning of the 1950s represented a continuation of old policies and social practices based on segregation and Jim Crowism, even though significant steps had been taken in the 1940s to break down the walls of prejudice and exclusion. The 1944 *Smith v. Allwright* decision had declared the "white primary" unconstitutional in three Southern states, allowing blacks to utilize their votes once again. The military also was changing some of its practices of segregation, but such changes were few and far between. Blacks remained the victims of racist practices in the workforce, where factory jobs and other positions were denied them in favor of white workers. In addition, entire neighborhoods were closed to black residents. Some whites were becoming staunch, hard-shell opponents of desegregation, and others were concerned that blacks were gaining too much power and that their "white supremacy" was being threatened, particularly by militant blacks who were leading the vanguard in support of black rights and black equality.

Even access to good schools continued as an ongoing problem for the nation's blacks. Certainly the *Brown* decision in 1954 and the follow-up *Brown II* in May 1955 were important steps in the desegregation of America's schools, but the expected changes did not take place overnight or even within the decade of the 1950s. Some states, including Maryland, Kentucky, Delaware, Oklahoma, and Missouri, took significant steps to desegregate, but other state leaders continued to drag their heels, keeping the promise of desegregation out of the hands of whole populations of black students.

The NAACP, the national black organization that had been involved in the struggle to desegregate America's schools throughout the first half of the twentieth century, would be threatened in the aftermath of the *Brown* decision. By 1957, nine Southern states had filed legal suits against the NAACP in a coordinated effort to crush the hated black organization. Some white leaders, including a young Virginia minister named Jerry Falwell, claimed that the black group was part of a Communist conspiracy. Several Southern states passed laws to outlaw the organization. NAACP membership dropped dramatically, from nearly 130,000 to fewer than 80,000 members. Throughout the South, nearly 250 local chapters of the organization were forced to close their doors. Prior to 1958, 13 U.S. school systems had desegregated. Two years later, as a new decade began, only two others had been added to that number. Despite the Supreme Court's voice of authority, desegregation in America's schools had a long way to go.

BUSES IN MONTGOMERY

During the early 1950s, racial discrimination was never outside the daily experiences of the vast majority of blacks in the South. Segregation permeated their lives, kept them

A MURDER IN MONEY, MISSISSIPPI

Perhaps as the result of a backlash against a rising tide of black assertiveness, an event took place during the summer of 1955 that gained immediate national attention and shocked many moderate whites as well as a majority of blacks. That summer, Emmett Till, a 14-year-old, black Chicagoan, was visiting relatives in the rural Mississippi hamlet of Money. One day, on a dare from his young friends, Till entered the local Bryant's Grocery, bought a handful of candy, and, as he left the store, spoke just two words to the woman behind the counter, Carolyn Bryant, the wife of the storeowner: "Bye, baby."* Without realizing it, young Till had violated the accepted code of behavior between blacks and whites in the town of Money, Mississippi. The consequences were dire.

Just a few days later, Carolyn Bryant's husband, Roy, and his half brother J. W. Milan went out to the house of Moses Wright, Till's great uncle, and, in the middle of the night, snatched the young boy at gunpoint. It was the last time Till was seen alive by his relatives. His body was found in the local Tallahatchie River, weighted down by a large cotton gin fan. The young Chicagoan had been shot in the head. His

in line, showed them who was in charge, and served as a constant reminder that Southern law did not protect them. The laws kept black children from attending better schools, allowed restaurants to refuse them service, denied them a hotel room at the end of a weary day of travel, and sanctioned movie theaters and playhouses to provide less for the price of their ticket, relegating black patrons to the balcony, if they were allowed entrance at all. Public drinking fountains were not "public" to a town's or a city's black residents and visitors. Just using a restroom might be difficult for a black person, who was forced to find one whose door carried the right sign: "Coloreds Only." Such reminders were at every corner for Southern blacks. They body bore the bloody marks of having been tortured and lynched. Both Bryant and Milan were arrested and stood trial. Despite the evidence and the testimony of Moses Wright, the men were found not guilty by an all-white jury. Having been cleared of their crime, Bryant and Milan were free to brag about what they had done and even sold their story to *Look* magazine.

Because Emmett Till was a Northern black, his death did not go unnoticed, as was often the case when a lynching victim was a black from the South. Emmett's mother, Mamie Bradley, kept the image of her murdered son in the public eye by having his body displayed in an open casket during a public burial ceremony in Chicago. Thousands of supporters sent her cards and letters of sympathy. The Emmett Till lynching would have a tremendous impact on the budding civil rights movement of the mid-1950s. Many who had not spoken up or dedicated themselves to the cause of black equality took up the banner in the future and marched on behalf of the cause.

* Darlene Clark Hine, *The African-American Odyssey.* Upper Saddle River, N.J.: Prentice Hall, 2005, p. 515.

were a daily reminder of the prejudices that caused whites to view them as inferior.

In many cases, the laws and practices that kept blacks from enjoying the same privileges as whites centered on indignities that might be experienced by one person at a time, private discriminations that one experienced individually. There was, however, one common, if not universal, discriminatory practice that blacks were forced to experience in groups. For many it occurred on a daily basis. In the cities of the South, public buses were segregated. Many blacks had to rely on taking such buses to work, to visit a doctor, to see friends, to do business, or simply to travel from one part of town to another. Every time a black person boarded a city bus, he or she was reminded that segregation was ever-present. The indignity was constant, and the rules varied little from one city to the next:

> The city buses were a microcosm of this segregated society. Black passengers, after paying their fares at the front of the bus, had to leave it and re-enter through the back door. They were allowed to sit only in the rear, and had to give up their seats whenever a white rider was left standing. . . . Day by day blacks stood together in the rear of crowded buses while the agents of their indignity sat comfortably right in front of them.[30]

Despite the ways in which blacks were treated by those who operated the city bus lines, in many Southern cities, they were the most common passengers. City buses were dependent on the fares of blacks but bus drivers often acted as if blacks who rode on their buses were a problem. It should not be surprising, then, that, when blacks finally rallied around a common cause in the early 1950s, it would be in opposition to the ways in which they were treated over and over again when they rode city buses.

One of the first Southern cities where blacks began to protest bus segregation was Baton Rouge, Louisiana. In 1953, blacks in the city delivered a petition to the city council to change its bus policy. The proposal was simple: Blacks would still sit in the back of the buses, but seating would be first come, first served. There would be no seats actually reserved for whites. When the council voted for the new ordinance, it appeared to be a victory for the city's black bus riders.

City bus drivers chose to ignore the ordinance, and blacks organized a single day's boycott, refusing to ride the city's buses. Their efforts were thwarted, however, when the state's attorney general decided that the new bus ordinance was illegal. The old bus practices again became the law. Blacks throughout the city had had enough, however. Three months later, Reverend T. J. Jemison, a minister in Baton Rouge, led a weeklong bus boycott. This time, city officials responded positively and a compromise was arranged. Seating would still be first come, first served, but two side seats up front would be reserved for whites. The boycott was considered a success by Reverend Jemison and those who cooperated with it. They had challenged white authority and a small battle against segregation had been won. It was a lesson not lost on the black residents of another Southern city located 400 miles to the east: Montgomery, Alabama.

PROTEST IN MONTGOMERY

The Montgomery City Lines bus company was similar to that of other Southern systems. It was operated on the basis of segregation, with blacks expected to give up their seats to whites and enter the bus from the rear. The back of the bus was reserved for black patrons. The Montgomery system had another rule, though: Officially, "if there were no seats available for blacks to move back to as additional white passengers got on, blacks were not required to give up their seats."[31] Despite the policy, however, it was common for bus drivers to expect blacks to stand if a white passenger needed a seat and there were none left. If a particular bus driver had designated certain seats for white passengers, blacks might actually have to stand up even with some of the "whites only" seats still empty. Such seating designated by race made no sense in practice. Every day, on Montgomery's buses, 40,000 blacks paid 10 cents to ride on a bus, and approximately 12,000 whites paid their dimes. Black passengers outnumbered whites by more than three to one. After the Baton Rouge bus boycott, Montgomery blacks decided to openly defy the city's bus policies.

One of the leading protesters was Jo Ann Robinson, a black English professor at Alabama State College, an all-black institution. She had memories of an incident she experienced in 1949, when, while carrying Christmas presents onto a nearly empty Montgomery bus, she sat down in the wrong seat, drawing the anger of the bus driver, who threatened to strike her if she did not get up and move from her seat. She had never forgotten the indignity and fear she had experienced. In 1953, she decided to take a stand against the city's bus policy. When she and other black leaders, including Edgar Daniel Nixon, a former leader of the Montgomery chapter of the NAACP, met with city officials, they were politely listened to, but the bus policy remained the same. Only one concession was made for the black patrons: City buses would "stop at every corner in black neighborhoods, just as they did in the white sections of town."[32]

Robinson and her fellow protesters began to consider the possibility of a Montgomery bus boycott among the city's blacks. They were, however, uncertain that enough blacks in the city would cooperate with a call to refrain from riding the city's buses. A boycott had been called several years earlier by Reverend Vernon Johns, a Dexter Avenue Baptist Church minister, but that effort had failed. Robinson knew that for a bus boycott to be successful, it would have to be well planned and would require blacks to cooperate despite the possibility of being inconvenienced and of possibly losing their jobs because they could not get to work.

Robinson and the Women's Political Council, a local group formed by black professional women (Robinson was the organization's president), began to organize their protest. They knew that they needed someone to defy bus policies and then get arrested, creating a stir that would rally blacks throughout the city. They needed "someone who could not only withstand the scrutiny and anger of whites but who could inspire black Montgomery to take action."[33] Such a person could become a test case against the city's bus policy. E. D. Nixon, Robinson, and the local NAACP chapter hoped that their efforts could create a legal case that could wind up in federal court, where the bus policies could be declared unconstitutional.

There were several black passengers who were arrested and supported by the NAACP, but none gave Nixon enough confidence to pursue a case: "I had to be sure that I had somebody I could win with . . . to ask people to give us half a million dollars to fight discrimination on a bus line, I [had to be] able to say, 'We got a good leg in.'"[34] Eventually, Nixon decided to create a case rather than to wait for the right one to come along. He could not know in the spring of 1955 that someone he had worked with at the NAACP would become his test case. She was the local NAACP's Youth Council adviser, a 42-year-old woman named Rosa Parks.

QUIET, BUT STRONG-WILLED

Miss Parks "was a quiet but strong-willed"[35] lifelong resident of Montgomery who had grown up in the city when there was no high school available for black students. Her family had supported her attending a laboratory school at Alabama State College, the all-black institution where Robinson taught English. Despite her education, Parks had worked over the years as a seamstress. In later years, she had worked with the Montgomery chapter of the NAACP as a secretary and then as a counselor. Parks had experienced the wrong side of the Montgomery bus policy herself 11 years earlier: While in her early 30s, she had one day refused to board a bus through the back door. The angry bus driver, James F. Blake, ordered her off his bus and drove away, leaving her in the street, despite having paid her fare.

On December 1, 1955, Montgomery, Alabama, resident Rosa Parks refused to give up her seat to a white passenger on a city bus. Parks was subsequently arrested for violating the city's segregation policy, and her actions would lead to the Montgomery bus boycott. Parks is pictured here with her attorney E. D. Nixon on the first day of her trial to challenge segregation on the city's buses.

During the winter of 1955, Rosa Parks was working as a part-time seamstress for a downtown Montgomery department store. On December 1, a Thursday, Parks paid her fare and boarded a Cleveland Avenue bus at the corner of Court Square. What happened next would begin a chain of events that would lead to important changes in the city for her fellow blacks. Parks entered the bus aisle and selected a seat in the first row of the bus's middle section.

The middle section was open for blacks when no white passengers were left standing. The problem arose at the next stop, Empire Theater. There, several whites boarded the bus, taking all the whites-only seats and leaving one white man standing. The bus driver then told Parks, along with three additional black passengers who were sitting in the bus's fifth row of seats, to move to the back section of the bus so that the white passenger could sit. None of the passengers moved, and tensions soon rose.

The bus driver then addressed the black passengers, including Parks, stating, "You better make it light on yourselves and let me have those seats."[36] At that point, the other three black passengers cooperated and moved to the back. Parks moved slightly to allow one of the black passengers to move past her, but she remained firmly in her seat. The bus driver then addressed Parks directly. Parks later remembered his words: "When the driver saw that I was still sitting there, he asked if I was going to stand up. I told him, no, I wasn't. He said, 'Well, if you don't stand up, I'm going to have you arrested.' I told him to go on and have me arrested."[37] Parks "spoke so softly that Blake would not have been able to hear her above the drone of normal bus noise" but he had turned the engine off.[38] The bus driver was as good as his word: The police were summoned, and Parks was taken to jail in a police car. There, police officials booked her for the crime of violating a city law against integration. At the station, Parks asked if she could get a drink from a nearby water fountain. She was told she could not: The fountain was reserved for whites only.

E. D. Nixon soon received the news that Rosa Parks had been arrested for violating city bus integration policy. Nixon would come to the jail and post Mrs. Parks's bond so that she could go home until her trial was held. He then asked her an important question: would she give her permission to use her case to tear down the segregationist bus policies in Montgomery? At first, Parks was hesitant. She spoke with her husband and her mother, who had always worried about her daughter's working with the NAACP. You'll get yourself lynched someday, her mother had warned her. Still, Parks decided to allow her case to be used for the important bus issue.

Boycott in Montgomery

For all his intentions, Nixon was only a former head of the local chapter of the NAACP. He did not have a close enough relationship with several chapter leaders, some of whom did not respect him, given he only had a sixth-grade education. Nixon chose to bypass the NAACP chapter directly and to make his appeal of support to local ministers and preachers, many of whom were leading citizens in their neighborhoods. One of the first he contacted was Reverend Ralph Abernathy.

ORGANIZING A BOYCOTT

The 29-year-old Abernathy was the minister at the First Baptist Church. Once Nixon gained Abernathy's support, he was able to contact 18 additional Montgomery ministers, many of them friends of Abernathy. Nixon called them to a meeting on Friday evening, December 2. Parks had been arrested the previous evening. In the meantime, Jo Ann Robinson contacted the leaders of the Women's Political Council. They offered their support and advised Robinson to call for a citywide bus boycott on Parks's behalf, to begin the following Monday, the day of Parks's hearing before the court. Over the weekend, Robinson prepared 35,000 handbills that read:

> This is for Monday, December 5, 1955—Another Negro woman
> has been arrested and thrown into jail because she refused to get

up out of her seat on the bus and give it to a white person.
It is the second time since the Claudette Colvin case that
a Negro woman has been arrested for the same thing. This
has to be stopped. . . . The woman's case will come up on
Monday. We are therefore asking every Negro to stay off
the buses Monday in protest of the arrest and trial. Don't
ride the buses to work, to town, to school, or anywhere
on Monday.[39]

The handbills were passed out in every major black
neighborhood, left in churches, storefronts, schools, and
even taverns and bars. Even before the ministers met on
Friday evening, the word of the boycott was beginning to
spread. Many of the ministers took it up and promised to
give the campaign their support, even though half of their
number became frustrated and chose to leave the meeting.
Of those who remained, the majority promised that they
would include word of the boycott in their sermons on
Sunday. Meanwhile, Nixon contacted a reporter for the local
newspaper, the *Montgomery Advertiser*, and informed him of
the boycott. The boycott story ran on the front page of the
Advertiser's Sunday morning issue.

The idea of a citywide boycott of Montgomery's bus
system had received much support from individuals and
groups throughout the city in just a matter of a few days.
Organizers had lingering doubts, however. Such boycotts
had been called earlier and failed. What if the citizens of
Montgomery did not support this bus boycott? Much was
riding on the success of the city bus boycott, and every
black resident of the city knew it. On Sunday afternoon,
organizers of the strike were only slightly hopeful about the
strike's success. Some of those hopes were dashed on Sunday
evening, when the weather looked as though it was going to
change, bringing rain showers for Monday.

DAY OF RECKONING

At dawn on Monday morning, the sky was dark and filled with clouds. It was a perfect day to take the bus rather than to risk walking across town and being drenched by the rain. Overnight, the city police department had been feverishly preparing for what might happen the following day. Stories were circulating that some of the city's blacks had organized "goon squads" to keep blacks from riding the city buses on Monday. The chief of police ordered a pair of motorcycle cops to follow each city bus on its scheduled route. The city of Montgomery was prepared for whatever rioting and protests might take place. It would prove unnecessary. Come Monday morning, people watched from their homes and saw buses moving about the city with literally no passengers on them.

Among those who witnessed these events, the impact of the boycott was soon obvious. One such witness was a Baptist minister named Martin Luther King Jr. He was the new minister of the Dexter Avenue Baptist Church. That morning, King was at home having breakfast when his wife called him from the living room, advising Martin that he needed to come to the front window of their home to see what she had observed. As Reverend King joined his wife in the front room, they both watched a slow-moving city bus drive by. The bus was nearly empty. King would later observe, "I could hardly believe what I saw. I knew the South Jackson line, which ran past our house, carried more Negro passengers than any other line in Montgomery."[40] Not on this Monday morning. Then, as the Kings watched, a second empty bus passed by. The boycott, which had been called only a few days before, had gained support from the city's large black population.

To aid the success of the boycott, the 18 taxi cab companies licensed in Montgomery had agreed to pick up and deliver as many black passengers as they could handle throughout the day for the same fare that the passengers would have paid to ride the city buses: 10 cents. (There were, after all, more than 200 black taxi cab drivers in Montgomery.) Those who could not get rides chose to walk through the city, taking their lunches with them to work and moving about Montgomery's streets and avenues with a new spirit of community and cooperation. As the *Alabama Journal* reported, "Negroes were on almost every street corner in the downtown area, silent, waiting for rides or moving about to keep warm. . . . None spoke to white people. They exchanged little talk among themselves. It was an almost solemn event."[41]

KING TAKES THE LEAD

At the city courthouse, huge crowds of supporters gathered to find out the result of Rosa Parks' trial. She would emerge from her day in court having been found guilty of violating segregation laws. She was given a commuted sentence and was then ordered to pay a $10 fine, plus $4 in court costs. A meeting was called for Monday afternoon to discuss the day's events. To facilitate and organize that meeting, Reverend Abernathy proposed that a new group called the Montgomery Improvement Association be organized. In short order, the group selected Reverend Martin Luther King Jr. as its president. King was chosen because he was new to Montgomery, and Reverend Abernathy had been working hard to get him interested in doing civil rights work. King had always begged off, telling Abernathy that he "was too busy getting his church in order." King was, E. D. Nixon explained, "a very intelligent young man."[42]

Once King had agreed to take the leadership of the boycott, the immediate question was whether or not the boycott should continue beyond its first day. The boycott had received strong support that Monday, reflecting more

During the yearlong Montgomery bus boycott, hundreds of African Americans took to the streets each day to walk to work. Here, a group of black women walk along a Montgomery sidewalk in February 1956, two months into the strike.

unity than the city's black leaders had ever seen before. The discussion raised doubts among the ministers: What if it rained tomorrow? What if the police were called in to intimidate the boycotters? Wouldn't a continuation of the boycott be interpreted by whites as a "direct assault by blacks on the system of Jim Crow?"[43] A frustrated E. D. Nixon spoke up: "How do you think you can run a bus boycott in secret? Let me tell you gentlemen one thing. You ministers have lived off these wash-women for the last hundred years and ain't never done nothing for them. . . . We've worn aprons all our lives. It's time to take the aprons off. . . . If we're gonna be mens, now's the time to be mens."[44]

Unable to come to an agreement, the ministers concluded their meeting by deciding to wait until they met in the evening to make a decision. The evening meeting was held at the Holt Street Baptist Church, a large congregation in one of the city's black neighborhoods. Meeting there would keep blacks from having to walk through white neighborhoods. Reverend King was scheduled to speak for 20 minutes. He did not know it at the time, but he was preparing to give one of the most important speeches of his career.

As the time for the meeting approached, the church was packed with excited people. Cars filled the parking lot, and some people had to park blocks from the church. As one attendee described what he witnessed, "The Holt Street Baptist Church was probably the most fired up, enthusiastic gathering of human beings that I've ever seen."[45] At the appointed hour, those gathered in the church engaged in singing and prayer. Black leaders rose to rally those present, shouting, "Do you want your freedom?" The audience responded, "Yeah, I want my freedom!"[46] The spirit of excitement and hope filled the crowded sanctuary. Then, 26-year-old Martin Luther King Jr. took the podium. He was so new to the city that many people in attendance did not know who he was. Still, his words would prove inspirational. The young minister spoke of the need for continued action

After the first day of the Montgomery bus boycott on December 5, 1955, the young minister of Dexter Avenue Baptist Church agreed to serve as spokesperson for the movement. Although he was just 26 years old at the time, Martin Luther King Jr. wasted little time in establishing himself as a strong leader for the African-American community.

but said that all things must be done passively, without violence. Then, he delivered the heart of his message:

> There comes a time when people get tired of being trampled over by the iron feet of oppression. There comes a time, my friends, when people get tired of being flung across the abyss of humiliation, when they experience the bleakness of nagging despair. . . . We are not wrong in what we are doing. If we are wrong, the Supreme Court of

this nation is wrong. If we are wrong, the Constitution of the United States is wrong. If we are wrong, God Almighty is wrong.[47]

Throughout the church, the audience sat in agreement, punctuating King's words with applause. The loudest, most

REVEREND KING AND THE SPIRIT OF GANDHI

The Montgomery bus boycott of December 1955 would become one of the most important events in the civil rights movement of the 1950s. It would help to launch the public career of Reverend Martin Luther King Jr. then a young, new resident of the city. He would become not only one of the most important supporters of the boycott, but, in time, the national voice of the civil rights movement, as well.

From the beginning, Dr. King emphasized to those who supported the Montgomery bus boycott that all protests and defiance of city authority or bus policy must be made without the use of violence. King's insistence came not only from his reading of the Bible and the example of Jesus Christ, who typically lived a life free of violence and chose instead to "turn the other cheek," but also from a more contemporary example. One of Reverend King's nonviolent inspirations was the twentieth-century Indian leader Mohandas Karamchand "Mahatma" Gandhi.

Gandhi was the leader of a nationalist movement of the people of India, uniting them in a campaign for independence from colonial control by Great Britain. He was a staunch Hindu advocate of passive resistance and nonviolence against British authority. Gandhi based his philosophy of nonviolent confrontation on the concept of *satyagraha*. (He actually coined the word because no word in English explained his philosophy.) The word is derived from two Sanskrit words, *satya*, meaning "truth," and *agraha*, which translates as "effort or endeavor." Satyagraha was, for Gandhi, an effort to discover truth.

enthusiastic approval came when Reverend King intoned the words, "We will not retreat one inch in our fight to secure and hold onto our American citizenship."[48]

After King's speech, Rosa Parks was introduced to the audience, which gave her a standing ovation. Reverend

In his philosophy, Gandhi became convinced that "pursuit of Truth did not admit of violence being inflicted on one's opponent, but that he must be weaned from error by patience and sympathy."[*]

As a doctoral student at Boston University, King had read some of the writings of Mahatma Gandhi and was highly interested in the Indian leader's approach to British authority in his country. He learned even more from another minister, Reverend Glenn Smiley, as well as from a fellow divinity student, James Lawson, who had given much study to Gandhi and Indian pacifism. Although Gandhi had a crucial impact on Reverend King's philosophy in meeting the resistance of whites toward the Montgomery Improvement Association's demands, he was influenced to a greater degree by his reading of the Bible and of the life of Jesus.

During the days of the bus boycott, King emphasized to those who supported the movement that they needed to meet white abuse, criticism, and even hatred with Christian love. Gandhi had made the same emphasis in his teachings: "Love does not burn others, it burns itself."[**] To King, if a resister of the city's bus policies reacted with violence, he or she would only hurt the cause. King believed that it was important that the boycott have all the hallmarks of a righteous cause. Satyagraha, as well as the teachings of Jesus, would guide Dr. King throughout his career as a civil rights advocate and segregationist resister.

[*] "Satyagraha." Wikipedia. Available online at *http://www. en.wikipedia.org/wiki/Satyagraha*.

[**] Ibid.

Abernathy then spoke on behalf of the Montgomery Improvement Association. He explained the association's demands: that bus drivers treat black passengers with courtesy, that black drivers be hired on black bus routes, and that bus seating be "first come, first served" with blacks still sitting in the back and whites in the front. Having thrown down the gauntlet, Abernathy then asked for a vote of the people assembled. One by one, those in attendance began to stand, signifying their support for continuing the boycott. Within minutes, every seat in every pew in the Holt Street Baptist Church was empty. Outside the church, the thousands of gathered supporters shouted their approval. The Montgomery bus boycott would continue.

THE CITY RESPONDS

Despite the enthusiasm for continuing the boycott, many black supporters had serious questions about the police, the city's leaders, and the local chapter of the Ku Klux Klan. They knew that they would face serious opposition. There might even be violent confrontations. Just months earlier, a Montgomery police officer had shot a black bus passenger when he refused to leave a bus and enter through the back door. No one knew what might happen next.

On December 8, a week after Rosa Parks's arrest, Dr. King, representing the MIA along with attorney Fred Gray, met with city leaders and bus company officials. King presented the group's three demands and was met with immediate opposition on all three fronts. The bus company's attorney even claimed that the seating arrangement King was demanding was illegal under Alabama law. Gray assured him that that was not the case, telling him that such an arrangement was already in use in Mobile and other cities throughout the state. In fact, Mobile's city buses were operated by the same bus company that ran the bus system in Montgomery. Still, the bus company's attorney, Jack Crenshaw, would not agree to the MIA demands. "The only way that it can be done," he claimed, "is to change your segregation laws."[49] Perhaps one city commissioner, Clyde Sellers, spoke for more people than he realized. He was opposed to the demands and stated that, "if we granted the negroes these demands, they would go about boasting of a victory that they had won over the white people."[50] The vast majority of the whites in Montgomery felt the same way: Give the city's blacks a little, and they will only want more in the future. To drive the point of entrenchment home even further, another city commissioner indicated that the city's black taxi drivers would have to charge the expected minimum fare of 45 cents, instead of a dime, or face heavy fines.

This spirit of refusal to compromise, to agree to even basic justice and equality, would both infuriate and enlighten Reverend King at the same time. He had entered the meeting with the city expecting that an agreement would be reached on each of the MIA's demands. He emerged from it understanding that the struggle ahead of him was going to be about much more than the way in which Montgomery's city buses were operated. It was going to be a struggle against the larger issue of segregation.

From Montgomery to Little Rock

As the Montgomery bus boycott continued through the following days and then weeks, the city's black population remained enthusiastic. Problems plagued the boycott, however. The greatest problem was how black workers could get to work and other places around Montgomery without using the city buses for transportation. Because the taxi drivers could not continue to charge a mere dime for a fare, they were not available to those who needed cheap rides. The answers soon came. People throughout the city—black and white together—rallied to provide the means to regularly traverse the city. Hundreds of people volunteered the use of their personal cars by carpooling. Jo Ann Robinson was one. The MIA organized a transportation committee to work out a system to move people around, getting help from black postal workers who had direct knowledge of the layout of streets in Montgomery. The committee bought several roomy station wagons and converted them into "taxis," which they called "rolling churches."[51] They established nearly 50 dispatch stations, along with 42 pickup sites. To keep supporters' spirits high, regular meetings were held twice each week, on Mondays and Thursdays.

THE BOYCOTT ROLLS ON

Additional support came to the MIA and the bus boycotters. Financial contributions rolled in from black people who could afford to give a dollar or two, as well as from wealthier black citizens. Whites contributed, too, although often anonymously. Montgomery's Jewish community gave money and, as the boycott dragged on, contributions from Northern supporters reached the coffers of the MIA. E. D. Nixon, who was the president of the Montgomery chapter of the Brotherhood of Sleeping Car Porters, got financial support from Detroit's United Automobile Workers. All donations were badly needed: The MIA-organized carpools were costing $2,000 per week.

As the boycott continued, city officials tried everything imaginable to deter the MIA's agenda. The police harassed many people, tried to pressure black taxi drivers, and gave support to the Ku Klux Klan, which organized violence against the boycotters. In January 1956, Montgomery city commissioners even tried to plant a false news story in the *Advertiser's* Sunday edition that claimed the boycott had ended. The following month, a grand jury in Montgomery indicted 89 individuals, including Dr. King and two dozen other ministers, on a charge of conspiring to boycott. That desperate move brought the Montgomery boycott to the attention of the national press. During the trial, interested people throughout the country got their first look at the defiant Reverend Martin Luther King Jr., the first "conspirator" to be put on trial. King was found guilty, fined $500, and sentenced to more than a year in jail. The judge, however, commuted his sentence because King had not incited any violent actions against the bus company or the city.

The boycotters remained determined to continue their efforts. Dr. King continued to provide inspiration, reminding those who cooperated with the boycott that the struggle was not "between the white and the Negro" but "between justice and injustice."[52] King continually worked to elevate the efforts of the boycotters as much as possible, giving them lofty goals that went far beyond where they might sit on a city bus in the future. His leadership of the boycott would cost him, as well as several of his coleaders, personally: Dr. King's home was firebombed, as were E. D. Nixon's, Ralph Abernathy's, and several other black ministers'.

So determined were the supporters of the boycott that it stretched into weeks and then into months. The hardship was carried especially by black women who had previously relied on the buses to get them to work. Some were aided by their white employers, who picked them up and delivered them home every day. Others had to walk as far as 12 miles to their jobs. The boycott was having exactly the impact that King and others wanted, though. The bus company faced severe losses of revenue because two of every three previous regular bus riders were no longer using the system. Bus drivers were laid off, schedules were shortened, and bus fares were raised. White shopkeepers and storeowners were hit hard, too, as their business dropped precipitously.

Although the bus boycott was hitting many in the pocketbook, it would not be enough to end the restrictive Jim Crow laws that the antagonistic bus policies were based on in the first place. That would require a legal battle in the courts. To that end, on February 1, 1956, MIA attorney Fred Gray, along with NAACP lawyers, filed suit against the bus company on behalf of five women who considered themselves victims of the bus policy. That June, a Montgomery federal district court decided two to one in favor of the women. The city appealed the case to the U.S. Supreme Court. Months later, on November 13, the highest court in the land decided the case titled *Browder v. Gayle,* ruling on behalf of the boycotters and ordering the city to end its policy of bus segregation. Suddenly, blacks in the city of Montgomery ecstatically rejoiced, having won a significant victory through the courts. In the weeks that followed, Montgomery's buses would roll again, with black passengers sitting anywhere they chose. The city and bus company also agreed to use black bus drivers. The date was December 21, 1956. The boycott had lasted 381 days.

FOUNDING THE SCLC

The end of the Montgomery bus boycott served as a wonderfully symbolic Christmas present to black supporters

On November 13, 1956, the U.S. Supreme Court ruled that African-American riders could sit anywhere on Montgomery, Alabama, buses. Shortly thereafter, on December 21, the bus boycott had come to an end. Here, Martin Luther King Jr. (second row, left) and fellow civil rights leader Ralph D. Abernathy (front row, left) ride the newly integrated Montgomery buses on December 21, 1956.

NORTHERN FRIENDS OF THE MONTGOMERY BUS BOYCOTT

The success of the Montgomery Bus Boycott was largely due to the city's black residents who cooperated in spirit and action and refused for more than a year to ride on city buses whose policies were based on nothing short of Jim Crow segregation. The bus boycott also received support from those who not only did not live in Montgomery, but did not even live in the South. Two of the most important of those "outsider" supporters were Bayard Rustin and a successful Jewish lawyer named Stanley Levinson.

Bayard Rustin was in his mid-40s in 1956. He was born in Pennsylvania and was a cofounder of the Congress of Racial Equality (CORE). A lifelong pacifist, Rustin had served three years in prison for refusing to participate in World War II when he was drafted. During his prison experience, Rustin more fully developed his philosophy of passive resistance.

Rustin helped encourage King's antiviolent approach to the boycott. He was a devoted follower of Gandhi's satyagraha. Approximately 10 weeks into the boycott, Rustin came to Montgomery and encouraged King and others to continue to embrace passivism. He would become one of Reverend King's most important counselors regarding nonviolent practices and tactics. When city officials harassed black leaders of the boycott, Rustin encouraged the leaders to surrender themselves to authorities. Several, including King and Nixon, did.

Stanley Levinson supported the boycott in a different way, although he was a friend of Rustin's. He was a wealthy lawyer who spent much of his legal career in the battle to achieve social justice for disenfranchised Americans, especially minorities. Levinson and an associate organized a group called In Friendship, which became a fund-raising effort to raise money to support the boycott.

of the boycott. After a full year of resisting white authority, the Supreme Court had finally ruled against the segregationist policies of the city officials and the bus company. The victory in Montgomery would have a greater impact on the future of blacks throughout America, however. The boycott would serve as a blueprint and a symbol for even more protests and future steps by which blacks would do damage to Jim Crowism. Several factors had made the Montgomery protest successful, and the lessons were not lost on those who watched as bus policy was changed. Those factors included capable and dedicated black leadership that received advice from the outside and had utilized a sympathetic national press to its advantage. In addition, the boycotters had used America's courts on their own behalf.

During the remainder of the 1950s, black organizers and leaders set a course for a larger civil rights movement in the United States. Each victory was important, each representing another step taken toward achieving equality. Civil rights leaders wanted to take their cause to the nation, though, and for that they needed a charismatic leader, someone who would have the respect of both the black community and the moderate white community. Reverend Martin Luther King Jr. had proven himself to be such a leader during the Montgomery bus boycott. Perhaps he could fill the role of the national spokesman that the civil rights movement so desperately needed.

King had certainly emerged from the boycott as not only a local hero, but as a voice with national resonance. After the successful boycott, King, along with several close associates, including Stanley Levinson and Bayard Rustin, took steps to form a new civil rights organization known as the Southern Christian Leadership Council (SCLC). The goals of the organization were to keep the flame of civil rights burning and to widen its scope. It represented a collection of civil rights groups, churches, and community-based organizations, all in need of a central organizational umbrella that could coordinate their individual efforts and goals. The Montgomery minister began to travel throughout the country working to strengthen the organization while also taking pains to raise as much money as possible for the group. The organization became a voice on college campuses throughout the United States, training potential civil rights activists, mainly college students, while continuing to emphasize King's antiviolence philosophy. In time, King would move his headquarters to Atlanta, Georgia.

One of the main tactics used by the SCLC was to secure voting rights for as many blacks as possible. The organization believed that voting was the key to much of the civil rights agenda, which called for complete school desegregation, equal employment opportunities, better housing, and equal access for minorities to public accommodations. SCLC representatives taught blacks in many communities how to organize their own civil rights efforts against Jim Crow bus policies. Soon, school bus segregation was challenged in Tallahassee, the capital of Florida, as well as in Atlanta.

The organization of the SCLC proved to be a problem for some members of the NAACP. Although both organizations backed a wide variety of the same goals for America's blacks, rivalry and tension grew between them. NAACP leaders were tepid concerning some of the tactics used by the SCLC, and sometimes the NAACP's legal wing was forced to take its attorneys off important court battles to defend SCLC members who were arrested during civil rights protests. The NAACP was also concerned with the possible connections between some of King's advisors and the American Communist Party. The SCLC arrived on the scene just in time, though: Because of white pressure in the South, some of it aimed directly at the NAACP, membership in the organization dropped significantly, sometimes leaving the SCLC as the only viable black civil rights organization in some regions of the South. Over the years, the NAACP and the SCLC continued to try to work together, but "tensions over tactics were never far from the surface."[53]

A NEW CIVIL RIGHTS ACT

During the months after the Montgomery bus boycott, the U.S. Congress continued to show support for the nation's blacks. In a show of support for the Supreme Court's *Brown* decisions, Congress passed the Civil Rights Act of 1957. This was the first significant civil rights legislation since Reconstruction had ended 80 years earlier, and it was a highly important and symbolic gesture on behalf of Congress. Its centerpiece was a commission whose purpose was to track alleged civil rights violations against blacks. Under this new act, the Justice Department had the power to file suits against both state law and local or municipal laws that were prejudicial. The Civil Rights Act of 1957 was not all it was touted to be, though. Many blacks worried that the act would not be enforced, especially by the federal government, because President Dwight Eisenhower did not go out of his way to actively support the tenets of the act.

TROUBLE IN LITTLE ROCK

Despite his lukewarm response in supporting the *Brown* decisions, President Eisenhower could not ignore events that unfolded in 1957 in Little Rock, Arkansas. That fall, steps were made to allow nine black students to enter Little Rock's Central High School, a formerly all-white school. School integration in Arkansas was not a new concept in 1957 and had actually begun prior to the initial 1954 *Brown* decision. The University of Arkansas at Fayetteville had voluntarily moved to integrate in 1948, and the university medical school in Little Rock had followed suit. (By the early 1950s, half of the students enrolled at Little Rock's state university campus were black.) Blacks in Arkansas had already taken dramatic steps toward integration, beginning in the mid-1940s. Blacks were on the Little Rock police force, several neighborhoods in the city were already integrated, and the city's parks, public transportation, and library were used equally by blacks and whites. Many of the state's eligible black voters were already registered. The Little Rock school board was, in fact, "the first in the South to issue a statement in compliance after the Supreme Court's ruling."[54]

LITTLE ROCK CENTRAL HIGH

RAY ROBERTS PATTILLO THOMAS WALLS

MOTHERSHED BROWN ECKFORD GREEN

On September 23, 1957, the Little Rock Nine—Gloria Ray, Terrence Roberts, Melba Pattillo, Jefferson Thomas, Carlotta Walls, Thelma Mothershed, Minnijean Brown, Elizabeth Eckford, and Ernest Green—became the first African-American students to attend Little Rock Central High School. The group was escorted to the high school by Little Rock police but they quickly departed after an angry white mob threatened to riot.

Yet, as the school session opened, Arkansas governor Orval Faubus defied the Supreme Court and placed 270 Arkansas National Guard troops around Central High to intimidate blacks from entering the school. To many, the move was a curious one because Faubus had been elected in 1954 as a liberal who promised to increase spending on schools and roads. During the early months of his administration, he had desegregated state buses and public transportation. He had even begun to study procedures for creating desegregated schools in his state. He had also helped pass a controversial tax bill to raise Arkansas teacher salaries earlier in 1957. (Some critics of Faubus claim that he denied blacks entry into Central High to gain political support across the state and to take the heat off of himself regarding the highly unpopular teacher pay increase. Also, one of his chief political rivals, James Johnson, had gained popularity in the state for leading the drive against integration.)

Faubus's decision to block the schoolhouse door to a handful of black students would not be ignored by President Eisenhower. When a federal district court ordered the governor to remove the National Guard troops, he complied but did nothing to provide protection for the would-be students. Instead, they were subjected to threats and intimidation at the hands of an angry mob opposed to school integration. On the morning of September 23, the nine students—people referred to them as the Little Rock Nine—arrived at Central High with a police escort. As the students walked toward the school, pandemonium broke out: Hundreds of white segregationists shouted at the children and began to throw objects. Someone mistook a black reporter at the scene for a parent of one of the children and threw a brick at him, hitting him on the side of his head. As the children reached the entrance to the school, whites shouted and cursed at them. Some in the angry mob began to cry when the black students actually walked over the threshold into the school.

A PRESIDENT INTERVENES

The next morning, another indignant crowd greeted the students. Governor Faubus was out of the state attending a Southern governors' conference at a resort in Sea Island, Georgia. Little Rock mayor Woodrow Mann doubted the capacity and resolve of the city's police to protect the black students and telephoned the U.S. Justice Department to ask for federal protection in the form of troops. The word reached President Eisenhower. He was fed up with Faubus, who had allowed white mobs to continue to threaten the black students. The president was not anxious to commit federal troops, but he felt that the crisis was no longer "an issue of racial integration but of insurrection."[55]

Speaking to his attorney general, Eisenhower made his decision: "Well, if we have to do this, and I don't see any alternative, then let's apply the best military principles to it and see that the force we send there is strong enough that it will not be challenged, and will not result in any clash."[56] That evening, he ordered more than 1,000 riot-trained troops of the 101st Airborne Division to fly from Kentucky to Little Rock Air Force Base to help defend the right of the Little Rock Nine to attend Central High. Arkansas National Guardsmen were also ordered to mobilize. Faubus had previously used them to keep the black students from entering the school, and they would now be expected to protect the same students. President Eisenhower also went on national television to explain to the American people why he had decided to call up federal troops. In his televised address, the president informed viewers that "disorderly mobs have deliberately prevented the carrying out of proper orders from a federal court."[57] Eisenhower, who had hoped that the *Brown* decision could be enforced without confrontation, made his commitment to the Little Rock situation even clearer:

> This morning the mob again gathered in front of the Central High School of Little Rock, obviously for the purpose of again preventing the carrying out of the court's order relating to the admission of Negro children to that school. Whenever normal agencies prove inadequate to the task . . . the president's responsibility is inescapable. . . . I have today issued an executive order directing the use of troops under federal authority to aid in the execution of federal law in Little Rock. . . . Mob rule cannot be allowed to override the decisions of our courts.[58]

The next morning, federal troops thronged around Central High and formed a protective ring. Three hundred uniformed and armed paratroopers were in formation along Park Avenue directly in front of the school. One of the black students, Ernest Green, remembered the sight that morning: "There was more military hardware than I'd ever seen. . . . The colonel in charge of the detail escorting us to school was from South Carolina. He had a very thick southern accent. He went to great pains to assure [the students' parents] that he was there to provide protection."[59] Green remembered having doubts about whether a white Southerner could provide him with much protection in the face of an angry white mob. When a dozen paratroopers advanced on the jeering white throng with fixed bayonets, however, the mob ran off. "The troops were wonderful," recalled another student, Melba Pattillo. "They were disciplined, they were attentive, they were caring, they didn't baby us, but they were there."[60]

The use of federal troops at Central High in Little Rock was the first time soldiers had been used to protect black citizens in the South since the days of Reconstruction. The troops remained at the school for the remainder of the school session. Single incidents of harassment continued, but thanks to their perseverance (eight of the nine stuck with it through the entire year despite their treatment by whites in the school), the integration of Central High in Little Rock became an important symbol in the fight for civil rights. The valiant behavior of the black students would be an inspiration to black students in other schools throughout the United States. Such courage paid off eventually. On May 29, 1958, Ernest Green became the first black student to graduate from Little Rock Central High School.

Despite his best efforts, Governor Faubus had been unable to keep blacks from becoming part of the student body at a high school in Little Rock. Still, he did not end his campaign against federal authority. In 1958, he closed Little Rock's public schools. As a result, approximately half of the city's white students enrolled in private schools instead. Others attended schools outside the city, and nearly 700 whites did not attend school anywhere. The same would be the case for most of the city's black high school students. Faubus's desperate move did not stop the advance of desegregation law, however. The Supreme Court ordered the schools to be reopened, referring to Faubus's tactic as just another of his "evasive schemes," as well as unconstitutional. By the fall of 1959, the city's public high schools were reopened. The conflict between a state official who defied the judicial authority of the Supreme Court and the executive authority of a U.S. president had ended with justice prevailing.

7

Standing Up by Sitting Down

The 1950s would conclude with the extended drama in Little Rock. A new decade of commitment to the civil rights movement in the United States was about to begin. Difficult times had marked the movement during the previous decade, but the future would witness even greater clashes and confrontations as civil rights leaders began to pursue different strategies. The efforts of those who fought for the cause of equal rights and privileges for the nation's black population paved the way for greater achievements. In fact, during the early years of the decade (1960–1963) "the civil rights movement developed the techniques and organization that would finally bring America face to face with the conflict between its democratic ideals and the racism of its politics."[61]

THE MOVEMENT'S IMPACT

The civil rights movement was already having a direct impact on national politics, which was evident in the presidential election of 1960. One concern of many Southern whites who watched the movement develop was that blacks might become better organized politically and begin to influence elections and ballot issues. That year, early in the presidential race, many blacks appeared to give their support to Richard Nixon, the Republican Party candidate, who campaigned in support of significant civil rights legislation. (Jackie Robinson, one of the great black baseball stars of the era, was a Nixon supporter.) In comparison, the Democratic Party's standard bearer, Massachusetts senator John F. Kennedy Jr. had done and said little in support of the ongoing campaign for black civil rights. As the election drew closer, however, Kennedy made "more sympathetic statements in support of black protests," whereas Nixon said less, concerned that he might lose votes among white Southerners.[62] Then, just prior to the election, Kennedy contacted Dr. King's wife, Coretta Scott King, and gave her his support when her husband was sentenced to a four-month jail term for his involvement in protests in Atlanta. That, combined with the efforts of Kennedy's brother Robert, who used his influence to help gain King's early release, swayed many blacks. Black support for Kennedy in many American cities helped win him the election. In the White House, though, Kennedy would not always prove to be an enthusiastic supporter of several of the tactics used by civil rights leaders to gain public approval for their cause. One of those types of confrontational tactics was being employed even before Kennedy took office.

SITTING DOWN IN WOOLWORTH'S

In 1960, a unique strategy against segregation was used for the first time in nearly 20 years. Black college students copied a tactic used by CORE in the 1940s. It was called the sit-in, and it would become one of the most important tools used against Southern segregation. It helped to speed up the social change needed to advance black civil rights.

This new generation of black protesters was led by college students. At 4:30 in the afternoon of February 1, 1960, four freshmen at North Carolina Agricultural and Technical College (A&T)—Ezell Blair Jr., Joseph McNeil, Franklin

On February 1, 1960, four African-American students from North Carolina A&T University organized a sit-in at the city's Woolworth's five-and-dime store to protest the store's segregated lunch counter. Pictured here during the second day of the protest are Joseph McNeil, Franklin McCain, William Smith, and Clarence Henderson.

McCain, and David Richmond—defied the segregationist policy of local restaurants in Greensboro by sitting down at a lunch counter in the city's Woolworth's five-and-dime store. It was the policy of the store to allow blacks to buy merchandise but not to sit at the lunch counter. The four freshmen sat at the counter, and those who worked behind it refused to offer them service. One of the young black men had ordered a cup of coffee from the lunch counter's white waitress, but she informed them that the lunch counter did not serve blacks.

"You just finished serving me at a counter only two feet from here," noted one of the black men, Ezell Blair. His response was unimportant to the waitress, who merely pointed the group of black men to the opposite end of the lunch counter, where they would be allowed to order food for take-out only. Blair continued to question the waitress: "What do you mean?" he asked. "This is a public place, isn't it? If it isn't, then why don't you sell membership cards? If you do that, I'll understand that this is a private concern." It was then that another lunch counter worker, a black woman, spoke up angrily, addressing the black men: "You are stupid, ignorant! You are dumb! That's why we can't get anywhere today. You are supposed to eat at the other end."[63]

The white manager at the counter did nothing overt to remove the young men. The four protesters remained at the counter, working on their homework, until the discount store closed its doors that evening at 5:30 P.M.

Word of their protest soon spread, and the following day, others joined them, including William Smith and several female students from Bennett College, Clarence Henderson, and a handful of white students from the University of North Carolina Women's College. What had started as 4 protesters had become 20 in just 24 hours. By day five of the sit-in, hundreds of black students, courteous and nicely dressed, crowded the downtown Woolworth's, intent on gaining the right to be served food at the establishment just like any white patron.

The first of those to engage in the Woolworth's sit-in did not make their decision to do so without devising a strategy. Blair, McNeil, McCain, and Richmond were not only insightful college students, they were also NAACP members who knew the stakes, knew the law, and wanted to strike a serious blow to at least one element of Southern segregation. In addition to those who flocked to Woolworth's to give them support, countless people, black and white alike, began sit-ins of their own at stores in the South that practiced segregation. Less than two weeks after the initial sit-in in Greensboro, a group of students in Nashville, Tennessee, who had been planning sit-ins of their own by engaging in practice workshops moved into action. Hundreds of demonstrators participated in sit-ins in several business establishments, leading some major restaurants to desegregate within a few months of the Greensboro sit-in.

NEW SIT-INS

With the success of the sit-ins in Greensboro, the civil disobedience tactic expanded, reaching Atlanta, Nashville, and Jackson. In all, approximately 60 Southern cities and towns were targeted for sit-in protests. With segregation on many different fronts to contend with, civil rights leaders established other forms of protest: Members participated in "wade-ins at segregated beaches, read-ins at segregated libraries, kneel-ins at segregated churches, walk-ins at segregated theaters and amusement parks."[64] There appeared to be no end to the scope of the sit-in movement so that "by the end of February sit-ins had been initiated by black college students across the South."[65]

In Atlanta, sit-ins became the new tactic against segregation. The initial inspiration for the protesters in Atlanta was a freshman at Spelman College, Ruby Doris Smith, who talked her friends into participating in a sit-in. In March, students at Morehouse College, including Julian Bond and Lonnie King, led a series of well-planned, massive sit-in demonstrations in the Atlanta area. Two hundred people fanned out and targeted 10 eating establishments in the city. They sat down at lunch counters in government buildings, public places, bus stations, train stations, and even the state capitol. Julian Bond would be arrested along with

PRACTICING FOR A SIT-IN

When four black college students engaged in a sit-in at the lunch counter at the Woolworth's in Greensboro, North Carolina, in 1960, they were doing so on their own, without outside incentive. The sit-in idea they utilized to protest segregation was not new; it had been used sporadically during the 1940s. As the four protesters sat down at the lunch counter of their choice, others had been planning, even practicing, to carry out the same kind of protest in their own communities.

In 1958, black civil rights leaders in Nashville, Tennessee, including Glenn Smiley, who had worked alongside Reverend King during the Montgomery bus boycott, began a series of workshops to help protesters, both black and white, learn the tactic of passive resistance. Within two years, such workshops had been established on black college campuses throughout the South.

One of the valuable lessons of such workshops was to remind a would-be protester, especially one who was black, "that nonviolence was not for the faint of heart."* Participants were required to sit passively while other students, role-playing as segregationists, shouted and mocked them. The passive protesters were forced to endure being struck, poked at, and even spat on.

The message was clear: that taking the moral high ground by protesting passively required much emotional and physical restraint, as well as discipline and the courage to remain loyal to one's own values. One workshop participant later remembered how she was taught to deal with

others after trying to eat at the cafeteria in the city's municipal building. After only a few hours in jail, Bond and the others were released. During the following months, protesters who engaged in sit-ins widened their targets to include "all public facilities, black voting rights, and equal access to educational and employment opportunities."[66] Despite the risks, many sit-in demonstrations did yield results. By late September 1961, more than 18 months after the first protest at the opponents while engaging in passive resistance: "I remember we used to role-play, and we would do things like pretend we were sitting at lunch counters, in order to prepare ourselves to do that. We would practice things such as how to protect your head from a beating, how to protect each other."**

The workshops employed an activity called "testing the lunch counters." This would require workshop teams to go to actual business establishments, such as department store lunch counters, to see if they would be denied service. If they were, they would typically ask to see the store manager and engage him in dialogue, telling him that it was wrong to discriminate against the members of a particular race based solely on the color of their skin.

In time, an organization called the Nashville Student Movement was established to create guidelines for each group of protesters to follow. The group members targeted specific retail stores. Part of their plan was to send a small group of college protesters into a store and sit at a lunch counter. Before the Nashville participants decided when to take their first overt steps to challenge segregation, Ezell Blair Jr., Joseph McNeil, Franklin McCain, and David Richmond had carried out a similar protest against the Greensboro Woolworth's.

---

* Juan Williams, *Eyes on the Prize: America's Civil Rights Years, 1954–1965.* New York: Penguin Books, 2002, p. 123.
** Ibid., p. 126.

Greensboro Woolworth's, Atlanta businesses and shops agreed to provide equal service to blacks.

One reason for the sit-in strategy's success was due to the number of participants. Within the first two months after the Greensboro sit-in, 2,000 people had participated in sit-ins, many of them having attended black high schools and colleges. By the summer of 1960, changes had been established or were underway in 30 Southern cities to respond positively to the pressures brought forth by the sit-ins.

ESTABLISHING THE SNCC

Much of the success of the sit-in movement hinged on the participation of college and university students who were willing to go to jail for the sake of a simple right such as eating at a public lunch counter. These students had played such an important role that steps were taken to ensure

Established in 1960, the Student Nonviolent Coordinating Committee (SNCC) was one of the primary civil rights organizations that participated in the Freedom Rides. Here, Martin Luther King Jr. addresses a group of SNCC members in Atlantic City, New Jersey, in August 1964.

their continued involvement in the civil rights movement. To that end, longtime civil rights campaigner Ella Baker, who ran the Atlanta chapter of the Southern Christian Leadership Council, established a new organization, one tailored for college student involvement. Called the Student Nonviolent Coordinating Committee (SNCC), the organization encouraged "the ideology of nonviolence, but it also acknowledged the possible need for increased militancy and confrontation."[67] Some civil rights leaders did not support the SNCC, fearing that the use of direct confrontational tactics against white authority would cause a backlash and that nonviolent means of protest would be replaced by this new form of resistance.

The SNCC might have caused some initial division within the civil rights movement, but no one could deny that the sit-in protests had been successful. In a sense, the confrontations at lunch counters led to yet another organized form of protest known as the Freedom Rides.

8

The Freedom Riders

In 1961, director of the Congress of Racial Equality, James Farmer and fellow CORE leader Bayard Rustin, resurrected an earlier strategy from the late 1940s that called for blacks to ride segregated trains and buses during interstate travel in the upper South. The earlier protest-on-wheels had failed miserably when the riders were arrested in North Carolina, convicted, and given monthlong sentences doing chain-gang labor. This time, the protesters hoped that they would receive greater support from the federal government and the Justice Department.

BOARDING FOR A CAUSE

As the sit-in movement had relied on direct confrontation, so would the Freedom Riders. The group's approach involved both blacks and whites: The white Freedom Riders would take seats in the back of buses, and black participants would sit in the front, a two-way violation of bus company policy. If ordered to move, both blacks and whites would keep their seats. At every bus stop, blacks would head for the whites-only waiting rooms and try to use the facilities. The strategy assumed that whites would respond violently and that such encounters could not be ignored by the federal government, or as James Farmer put it, "so that the federal government would be compelled to enforce federal law. That was the rationale for the Freedom Ride."[68]

The first group of "Freedom Riders" boarded a bus in Washington, D.C., on May 4, 1961. Thirteen riders had been recruited. The planned trip would take them through Virginia, North Carolina, and South Carolina and then across the Deep South to Louisiana. The group hoped to reach New Orleans on May 17, the seven-year anniversary of the *Brown* decision. Each of the riders knew the dangers involved in participating: "We were told that the racists, the segregationists, would go to any extent to hold the line on segregation in interstate travel," James Farmer noted. "So when we began the ride I think all of us were prepared for as much violence as could be thrown at us. We were prepared for the possibility of death."[69]

The first confrontation took place in a Greyhound bus station in Rock Hill, South Carolina. Seven blacks attempted to enter a whites-only portion of the terminal. One of them, John Lewis, was attacked and beaten as local police watched. Through Virginia and the Carolinas, the riders met repeated resistance, with scuffles taking place in bus station restrooms and at lunch counters. Still, the riders pressed on. Ten days into their trip, the group split up and continued from Atlanta to Birmingham, Alabama, on two different buses. The only stop before Birmingham was Anniston, Alabama. There, the Freedom Riders would encounter the most violent protests of their trip.

When the first bus of riders reached Anniston, whites who had gathered outside the Greyhound terminal began to throw rocks at the bus. Hundreds of angry protesters surrounded the bus, slashing its tires. The bus driver sped away from the scene of the attack and did not stop until he had driven six miles out of Anniston. When the bus driver stopped to fix the flat tires, the mob caught up with the bus and a firebomb was tossed through one of the windows. Passengers bolted for the emergency exit as the fire inside the bus spread. Suddenly, everything the Freedom Riders hope to achieve was coming to fruition. The media picked up the story, and the image of the burning bus could be seen on television and in newspapers throughout the contry. This image became yet another metaphor of the civil rights movement of the 1960s.

The second bus managed to reach the Trailways terminal in Birmingham safely, but an angry mob was waiting at the station. Shortly after the bus arrived, the mob attacked the second group of Freedom Riders. In the meantime, the city's public safety commissioner, Bull Connor, had not placed a single police officer at the terminal to keep the peace, although he knew the Freedom Riders were coming into Birmingham. (Connor claimed that he had sent no officers because it was Mother's Day and they were off duty.) With no one present to stop them, the mob attacked the Freedom Riders, leaving one, William Barbee, paralyzed for life.

Upon hearing what happened in Alabama, President John F. Kennedy Jr., only four months into office, called a meeting with his brother Robert, the nation's attorney general, and several Justice Department staffers. The group decided to prepare to send federal marshals to Alabama. Back in Alabama, other steps were also being taken. Greyhound officials, concerned about having one of their buses firebombed, decided to bar the Freedom Riders from using their buses. Suddenly, the Freedom Riders were trapped in Birmingham. Fortunately, they were able to get to a local airport and take a plane to New Orleans.

This, however, would not be the end of the Freedom Ride movement. Soon, 10 more Riders, fresh from Nashville and their involvement in sit-ins in the Tennessee capital, went

On May 4, 1961, the first Freedom Riders departed from Washington, D.C., and headed for New Orleans. During their trip, many were arrested for violating state and local Jim Crow laws. Here, a group of freedom riders waits near a bus in Birmingham, Alabama, after the bus driver refused to let them board the bus.

to Birmingham to take up the fight where the first group of Freedom Riders had been stopped cold in their tracks.

LEADERS SQUARE OFF

Attorney General Robert Kennedy had already sprung into action. He was intent on enforcing federal law in support of integration on interstate means of transportation, even though his calls to Alabama governor John Patterson had gone unreturned. (Patterson had publicly spoken out against the freedom riders, stating, "When you go somewhere

LIMITED SUPPORT FOR THE FREEDOM RIDERS

As blacks and sympathetic whites boarded Trailways and Greyhound buses during the summer of 1961, they were met, of course, by mobs of white Southerners who were angry that long-standing Jim Crow laws were being challenged. Some whites who watched the Freedom Rides on their television sets responded with quiet understanding and support, but many more throughout the country did not think that those riders who boarded Southern buses to force confrontation were pursuing the right strategy. In a Gallup poll taken that June, nearly two out of every three Americans, black and white alike, disapproved of the Freedom Rides.

Many members of the press were opposed to the confrontational rides, and support for the tactic was limited even in some newspapers that were generally supportive of the civil rights movement. The *New York Times*, "which gave King and the civil rights movement generally sympathetic coverage,"* did not want to see the rides continued after the bus burning in Anniston and clashes in Birmingham. The paper editorialized against the riders, declaring, "They are challenging not only long-held customs but passionately held feelings. Non-violence that deliberately provokes violence is a logical contradiction."** When King decided to support the continuation of the rides after the Birmingham violence, the *Times* again wrote negatively: "Some liberal Southerners of both races joined moderates and others today in asserting that the Freedom Riders should be halted."*** Intent on reducing the level of publicity for the riders, the *Times* kept the subject off its front page for the remainder of the summer.

looking for trouble, you usually find it."[70]) Attorney General Kennedy instead made calls to the Birmingham Police Department, as well as to the Greyhound Bus Company. When he received word that another group of Riders was on its way to Birmingham, Kennedy became concerned.

There was even a disappointing lack of support from the White House. Three weeks into the rides, on May 25, President John F. Kennedy delivered a speech to Congress, similar to a second State of the Union address. Although Kennedy alluded to freedom—"I am here to promote the freedom doctrine"[†]—he did not mean the Freedom Riders. His speech did not even mention the riders. Instead, he was intent on presenting to Congress an agenda that centered on other fights for freedom: "The great battleground for the defense and expansion of freedom today is the whole southern half of the globe—Asia, Latin America, Africa, and the Middle East, the lands of the rising peoples. Their revolution is the greatest in human history. They seek an end to injustice, tyranny, and exploitation."[††] As Kennedy used words such as "injustice" and "exploitation," he ignored racial injustice in the United States. The following month, at his next press conference, Kennedy still did not mention the Freedom Riders, even though hundreds had been jailed by then. The press did not ask him a single question about the riders, either.

Attorney General Robert F. Kennedy did try to work with King and the Freedom Riders and give them federal support. Still, the tactic of confronting white racism by riding buses from one Southern state to the next never did gain any significant support from the press, the presidency, or the American people.

---

[*] Taylor Branch, *Parting the Waters: America in the King Years, 1954–63*. New York: Simon and Schuster, 1988, p. 478.
[**] Ibid.
[***] Ibid.
[†] Ibid., p. 477.
[††] Ibid.

When the new Freedom Riders arrived in Birmingham, the city's police moved into action, simply choosing to arrest them. The Freedom Riders were told by Bull Connor that it was all for their own safety. On the night of May 17, the new Freedom Riders were jailed and immediately protested by embarking on a hunger strike. After two days of the hunger strike, Public Safety Commissioner Connor arrived at the jail to inform the Freedom Riders that he was having them taken back to Nashville. When the students refused to cooperate, they were forcibly taken from the jail, loaded into police cars, transported 120 miles to the Alabama-Tennessee state line, and dropped off beside the road. After they made phone contact with Diane Nash, a Nashville coordinator of earlier sit-ins and of the Freedom Riders, cars were sent to pick them up. The Freedom Riders were not going on to Nashville, however. They wanted to go back to Birmingham to the bus station. When they tried to board a bus, though, the white driver refused, stating, "I don't have but one life to give. And I don't intend to give it to CORE or the NAACP."[71]

Meanwhile, Governor Patterson called Robert Kennedy. The conversation was short and confrontational. Patterson would agree only to meet with a Justice Department aide named John Seigenthaler. His reason was that Seigenthaler was a fellow Southerner. The meeting between the two men was heated: Patterson intended to stand his ground, claiming that there would be "warfare" if Robert Kennedy sent federal officials to Alabama to protect the Freedom Riders.[72] Seigenthaler was equally adamant, stating clearly to the Alabama governor, "What I'm authorized to say is if you're not going to protect them, the federal government will reluctantly but nonetheless positively move in whatever force is necessary to get these people through. They've got to be given protection and so do other interstate passengers."[73]

At that point, Governor Patterson seemed to relent. He promised Seigenthaler that his state police would protect the Freedom Riders from Birmingham to Montgomery. From there, it would be up to the Montgomery police to provide protection. When Kennedy received word of Patterson's promise, he asked the governor to make a public statement, which Patterson agreed to. When Governor Patterson issued his official statement that promised to protect the Freedom Riders, he included the pointed line, "We don't tolerate rabble-rousers and outside agitators."[74] With Patterson's assurances, Kennedy called the superintendent of Greyhound's terminal in Birmingham and pressured him to allow the Freedom Riders to continue their trip to New Orleans. "I think you . . . had better get in touch with Mr. Greyhound, or whoever Greyhound is," said Kennedy, "and somebody better give us an answer to this question."[75]

Kennedy's pressure would pay off. A week after the firebombing of the Greyhound bus in Anniston, another busload of new Freedom Riders was headed for Montgomery under the protection of Alabama state police, which had promised that "a private plane would fly over the bus, and there would be a state patrol car every fifteen or twenty miles along the highway between Birmingham and Montgomery," a distance of less than 100 miles.[76] Onboard were two Greyhound officials. Justice Department official John Seigenthaler would drive a rental car directly in front of the bus. Everything appeared to be under control. Once the bus reached the Montgomery terminal, though, the state police left. Calm soon gave way to confrontation once again.

MAYHEM IN MONTGOMERY

In the terminal, chaos broke out as brick-wielding whites stormed the bus, shouting, "Niggers, kill the niggers."[77] The Freedom Riders were trapped in the bus. Three black riders managed to escape the bus and fled to a local post office. Seigenthaler, who had stopped for gas, drove up after the attack on the bus passengers had already begun. He drove his car straight into the angry mob, where he tried to help some of the Freedom Riders. Threatened himself,

Seigenthaler shouted, "Get back! I'm a federal man!"[78] He was struck from behind and rendered unconscious. The head of the Alabama State Police, Floyd Mann, was also in the station. Despite his orders to the mob to stop their attack, the angry whites continued to abuse the Freedom Riders with everything from baseball bats to pipes to their fists. Mann pulled out his service pistol and fired a shot into the air. Soon, the white mob scattered, leaving Freedom Riders wounded and bleeding, Seigenthaler unconscious, and several cars in flames. Mann ordered additional state troopers to the bus terminal and then called the governor. Martial law was immediately declared in Montgomery, Alabama. Word soon reached President Kennedy and his brother. They both knew that Governor Patterson had not protected the Freedom Riders. The president ordered 600 federal marshals to Alabama; they soon arrived at Maxwell Air Force Base outside Montgomery. Two hundred of them were dispatched to the hospital where the Freedom Riders were treated for their injuries. Governor Patterson publicly questioned the action by the president, stating, "We don't need your marshals. We don't want them, and we didn't ask for them. And still the federal government sends them here to help put down a disturbance which it helped create."[79]

With the confrontation escalating daily, evenly hourly, Reverend Martin Luther King Jr. flew into Montgomery and spoke at a rally in Ralph Abernathy's First Baptist Church the day after the attack. Twelve hundred supporters attended. King gave his support to the Freedom Riders as federal marshals formed a protective barrier around the church building. As King spoke, a crowd of several thousand whites showed up at the church and formed their own ring around the federal marshals. In many ways, Montgomery's whites had not put the days of the bus boycott behind them. They were still angry, and racial tension had led to the closing of all of the city's public parks, as well as the city zoo, just so blacks could not have the use of them. Years of racist frustration had finally exploded that very evening in May.

From outside, the white mob shouted insults and curses at the blacks gathered inside. At 3:00 A.M., an angry Reverend King made a call to Robert Kennedy, asking him what he intended to do about the mob that had trapped him and his audience in the church. "If [the marshals] don't get here immediately," an anxious King stated, "We're going to have a bloody confrontation. Because they're at the door now."[80] Kennedy responded directly: "I said that I didn't think that he'd be alive if it hadn't been for us, that we were going to keep him alive and that the marshals would keep the church from burning down."[81]

Robert Kennedy then telephoned Governor Patterson, but initially he seemed unable to get past the governor's anger at having federal marshals policing Montgomery. Meanwhile, those very marshals were clashing with the white mob outside the church. As angry Alabamans threw beer bottles, the federal marshals threw tear gas. When gas blew into the church, Reverend King tried to calm the crowd, telling them that it was not the time to panic. Governor Patterson did respond to the situation directly, sending in state police and even Alabama National Guardsmen, who first broke up the mob outside the church and then escorted Dr. King and the black attendees out of harm's way.

THE RIDES RESUME

Both the president and the attorney general hoped that the Freedom Riders would not abandon their mission to continue their ride to New Orleans. However, they called for cooler heads and an end to the confrontations. The Kennedys had grown tired of the conflict between Governor Patterson and the Freedom Riders, feeling that they were only escalating the clashes. The Freedom Riders had no intention of ending their drive for New Orleans, however. Two days after the confrontation outside the First Baptist Church, 27 Freedom Riders boarded two buses headed west toward Jackson, Mississippi. They asked Reverend King to join them on one of the buses, but the civil rights leader chose not to because he was still on probation for his involvement in the Atlanta sit-ins. He would be criticized for this decision.

The bus ride to the Alabama-Mississippi state line was without incident. Then, the Freedom Riders were overjoyed

When the Freedom Riders entered the state of Mississippi in late May 1961, they were overjoyed to find Mississippi National Guardsmen lining the highway to protect them from protesters. Unfortunately, when they reached the bus terminal in the state capital of Jackson, they were arrested by state police for trespassing.

when they saw Mississippi National Guardsmen lining the highway "with their guns pointed toward the forest on both sides of the road."[82] Robert Kennedy, in the meantime, tried to pave the way for the Freedom Riders through Mississippi. He had contacted U.S. Senator James O. Eastland to work out a deal. Kennedy promised the staunch segregationist he would not send in federal officials if Eastland would promise him that there would be no armed attacks against the Freedom Riders. Eastland assured the attorney general that there would be no violence in his state.

The armed guard extended to the outskirts of Jackson. Some of the Freedom Riders were singing, excited about the change in their prospects of reaching their final destination in New Orleans:

> I'm taking a ride on the Greyhound bus line.
> I'm riding the front seat to Jackson this time.
> Hallelujah, I'm traveling;
> Hallelujah, ain't it fine?
> Hallelujah, I'm traveling
> Down Freedom's main line.[83]

In Jackson, no mob had gathered to confront the Freedom Riders. The Freedom Riders were able to disembark in the terminal and even to use the whites-only waiting room, although they were escorted by policemen. Despite these positive signs, the Freedom Riders were quickly jolted back to reality. As they passed through the whites-only waiting room, state police quietly but firmly ushered them out of the station, into waiting police cars. They were being arrested for violating various state laws. There had been no violence in Mississippi, just as Senator Eastland had cynically promised.

With the arrest of the Freedom Riders under Mississippi law, Robert Kennedy could do little to protect them further. The Freedom Riders were hauled into court within 24 hours, summarily accused of trespassing, and sentenced to 60 days in a Mississippi state penitentiary. Although the Freedom Riders were jailed, additional Freedom Riders—at least 300 in all—took buses into Jackson through the following months. The vast majority of them were also arrested after entering the whites-only portion of the bus terminal. Robert Kennedy, in the meantime, worked with Interstate Commerce Commission officials to convince them to create more regulations concerning integration on buses and in bus terminals. The changes did not take place until September.

Through these tense spring and summer weeks of confrontation, violence, and bloodshed, the Kennedys had tried to give support to the Freedom Riders while also trying to keep Southerners within the Democratic Party happy. To that end, Robert Kennedy began to suggest that the students and other civil rights supporters might be better served by carrying out a grand campaign to increase black voter registration. "There wasn't going to be as much publicity about it," said Kennedy, "but I thought that's where they should go and that's what they should do."[84] At first, Kennedy's suggestion received a tepid response from civil rights leaders, including Dr. King. They thought that the attorney general was only trying to limit the scope of the civil rights movement for political reasons. The Kennedys did encourage support and donations to this movement. It would later be known as the Voter Education Project and would be headquartered in Atlanta.

In time, King and others came to believe that voter registration might yet be another important tool for the civil rights movement. It would not require a significant level of confrontation, and the potential for violence would be greatly reduced. In the following years, black votes would indeed help bring about change in American society.

The Freedom Riders had placed themselves in harm's way and had risked their lives for the sake of their political cause. They forced white segregationists to express their anger in dramatic ways, providing the civil rights movement with perhaps its highest level of national media attention ever. Pictures of a burned out, firebombed bus in Anniston, Alabama; of bruised and battered black college students, wounded by white rage; and hundreds of federal marshals protecting the lives of blacks trapped in a Baptist church had managed to convey to those watching the movement from the outside a more powerful message than could be delivered in a thousand words.

9

Getting Out the Vote

After the dramatic confrontation in May 1961 in response to the actions of the Freedom Riders, Robert Kennedy called for a meeting with student civil rights activists and leaders and pressured them to rechannel their efforts into increasing black voter registration. By the end of that summer, several civil rights organizations had agreed to work together toward this important political goal, one that could have long-term consequences and make significant inroads in achieving political and social goals for blacks. Leaders of the SNCC, the SCLC, CORE, and the NAACP pooled their resources, and, with the backing of several significant charitable organizations, sent their members out to get blacks registered to vote. Between them, they divided up the South; the Student Nonviolent Coordinating Committee took the responsibility of registering voters in Alabama and Mississippi. The SNCC created several "voter registration schools," where they trained volunteers to sign up potential black voters, in these states. These efforts would not go unnoticed by local whites, and violent confrontations once again broke out.

THE ALBANY SETBACK

When SNCC members tried to set up a major voter registration project in Albany, Georgia, during the summer of

1961, they were met with immediate obstacles and defiance by whites. Albany, located in southwestern Georgia, was a community of 56,000 residents, 40 percent of whom were black. It was the first Southern city the SNCC targeted, not only for voter registration, but also to rally local blacks on a number of other issues. The SNCC agenda in Albany that summer included challenging the segregationist policies of the local bus and train stations. When its volunteers tried to eat at the lunch counter in the local Trailways terminal, local police arrested them for refusing to obey a law enforcement official. The savvy Albany chief of police, Laurie Pritchett, knew to avoid any charges that might involve a federal crime, thus leaving national government officials out of the loop.

Other civil rights groups, including the SCLC, responded. In time, Dr. King and several hundred volunteers arrived in Albany, hoping to draw national media attention to the situation. By the time King and his volunteers arrived, there were already more than 500 civil rights advocates in jail in the Georgia community. On December 16, King would be counted among them. Within two days of King's arrest, officials for both the Albany movement and the city agreed to a truce and King was allowed to leave his jail cell and return to Atlanta. Once King was gone, however, city officials did not live up to their part of the bargain, forcing him to return to Albany. During the intervening months, into 1962, the conflicts in Albany remained unresolved and Dr. King found himself outmaneuvered at nearly every turn. When King's strategy relied heavily on filling the Albany jail with protesters, Pritchett simply contacted as many jails within 15 miles of Albany as he could to take the overflow, effectively deflecting King's primary tactic. In the end, the Albany experience would prove to be a failure for Reverend King, one of the few of his civil rights career and one that caused him to question whether the movement would continue to be successful.

In July 1962, SNCC members attempted to set up a voter registration project in Albany, Georgia, while also challenging other segregationist policies in the city. Here, Albany's chief of police, Laurie Pritchett, notifies African-American demonstrators that they will be arrested because they did not have a permit to organize.

In the spring of 1963, a discouraged King was concerned that the civil rights movement was at a crossroads and that it might fall apart. The movement had created strong and significant support and had many members who were willing to do whatever it took to support the cause. Changes were still being made on a modest level for the amount of effort that had been expended over the previous years, though. After all, nearly a decade had passed since the initial *Brown* decision and school integration had not yet been fully achieved. Although President Kennedy had shown some support for the movement, he "remained reluctant to act unless faced with open defiance by white people or televised violence against peaceful protesters."[85]

The Albany setback had been a rare defeat for the movement, and if other city leaders responded in the same ways—avoiding charges that violated federal law, refusing to rely on extreme responses that included violence, and even giving King an early pass out of jail—the movement might falter completely. To make certain that did not happen, King and the SCLC created yet another campaign in 1963. After all, that year did mark the one-hundredth anniversary of the Emancipation Proclamation.

RETURN TO BIRMINGHAM

The primary target for the campaign would be Birmingham. The city had already seen its share of civil rights conflict and confrontation and "was ripe for such a protest."[86] The city was notorious for the Mother's Day attack against the Freedom Riders in 1961. Racial strife had continued in Birmingham, which had seen 18 unsolved bombings in black neighborhoods between 1957 and 1963. This dubious distinction had earned the city the nickname "Bombingham." The previous year, white city officials had "closed sixty-eight parks, thirty-eight playgrounds, six swimming pools, and four golf courses to avoid complying with a federal court order to desegregate public facilities."[87] The Ku Klux Klan was extremely strong in the Birmingham area. Despite the high level of racism in the city, the Alabama Christian Movement for Human Rights (ACMHR), a local black organization, tried to stand its ground. It joined forces with the SCLC and together these organizations planned activities such as boycotts, demonstrations, and pickets. This movement went by the name Project C (the "C" stood for confrontation). The goals of the campaign included the integration of public facilities and public schools, employment opportunities for blacks, and low-income housing. The organizations hoped that their activities would encourage public safety commissioner Bull Connor, who had overreacted in earlier confrontations, to react violently again, drawing the attention of the American people and especially of President Kennedy, who would be compelled to respond on behalf of the federal government.

The project began on April 3, 1963, with college student-led sit-ins. Connor responded, but not with violence. When Alabama courts tried to ban such protests, reverends King and Abernathy participated in additional sit-ins and were arrested on Good Friday, April 12. Once again, a civil rights campaign in a Southern city was not succeeding as planned. Connor was not overreacting to the extent that the protesters had believed he would, and many of the protesters ended up in jail. A change in tactics, however, soon ensured success for Project C.

James Bevel, an SCLC official, suggested that black schoolchildren be used to protest. Although his suggestion was not fully accepted by all within the movement, King approved it as necessary for the good of the protest and for the future of the children in question. On May 2 and 3, the SCLC sent thousands of black children, some as young as six or seven, out into the streets of Birmingham to protest. Finally, Bull Connor had had enough.

Birmingham police went into the streets and began to arrest the children. Connor's crackdown included ordering firemen to turn their powerful hoses on the children. The highly pressurized hoses were "capable of knocking bricks loose from mortar or stripping bark from trees at a distance of one hundred feet. . . . The hoses made limbs jerk weightlessly and tumbled whole bodies like scraps of refuse in a high wind."[88] Then, Connor unleashed the K-9 units, and "growling German shepherds lunged toward stumbling, cowering stragglers. They bit three teenagers severely enough to require hospital treatment."[89] Television cameras were filming, and the American public was sickened by the sights.

Some of the children and their parents tried to fight back, throwing rocks and bottles at Birmingham police.

The violence drew other immediate responses. White Birmingham businessmen called for calm and encouraged the city to begin negotiations. President Kennedy sent Burke Marshall, a Justice Department official, to the race-torn Southern city to talk with officials. A week later, an agreement was made. White businesses would integrate their downtown stores and employ black workers. The agreement brought on another round of violence as Ku Klux Klan members firebombed the SCLC headquarters in the A. G. Gaston Motel, as well as a house owned by Reverend King's brother, A. D. King. In response, black protesters set fires in several buildings and cars and renewed their assaults on the police. Once Reverend King and several moderate white leaders in Birmingham intervened, the agreement remained intact. The campaign in Birmingham was not going to end as it had in Albany, Georgia.

The successes gained in Birmingham would prove to be a turning point in the civil rights movement of the 1960s, but it would come at a cost unforeseen that spring. Through the summer of 1963, protests spread across the South, with 800 marches, sit-ins, and rallies. Nearly a dozen civil rights workers would be killed, and 20,000 were arrested on every charge that racist Southern officials could imagine. One of those killed was Medgar Evers, an executive secretary of the NAACP in Mississippi, who was shot in the driveway outside his home on June 12. His killer was a local white supremacist, Byron De La Beckwith, who remained free after two trials ended with hung juries. In 1994, Beckwith was finally convicted and sentenced to life in prison.

NEW LEGISLATION

Despite these setbacks and continuing challenges to the movement, there was a bright spot that gave new hope to civil rights advocates. On June 11, partially in response to

DR. KING'S PRISON LETTER

When black and white protesters staged sit-in demonstrations in Birmingham, Alabama, in the spring of 1963, they were arrested by local police officials under the command of Public Safety Commissioner Bull Connor. Connor rounded up as many protesters as he could and had them arrested and put in jail. In time, Reverend Martin Luther King, Jr., along with Reverend Ralph Abernathy, was also arrested and jailed. King had been incarcerated previously for his civil rights activities, but this time he took the opportunity to write one of his most important movement-related documents.

After receiving criticism from eight Birmingham clergymen and Jewish leaders for what they thought were his "unwise and untimely" protests,[*] King felt compelled to write a response. Having hidden a pen during his booking, he collected slips of paper, including toilet tissue and a copy of the *Birmingham News* (contained the open letter criticizing King) and penned his response, which would one day be known as his "Letter from Birmingham Jail."

In this important civil rights document, King answered his critics by justifying his use of direct action. He was tired of those who thought that oppressed black Americans should just simply be more patient and wait for change to come on their behalf. "I guess it is easy for those who have never felt the stinging darts of segregation to say 'Wait,'" he wrote.[**] As he wrote, he stressed that "freedom is never voluntarily given by the oppressor; it must be demanded by the oppressed."[***] His words gave further meaning and context to the importance he placed on why he thought such protests were needed and why he encouraged nonviolence:

the horrors perpetrated in Birmingham by Bull Connor and others, President Kennedy announced his intent to present a new civil rights legislative package to Congress. The bill would include the integration of any publicly or privately owned businesses or facilities, including all

Nonviolent direct action seeks to create such a crisis and foster such a tension that a community which has constantly refused to negotiate is forced to confront the issue. It seeks so to dramatize the issue that it can no longer be ignored. . . . Any law that degrades human personality is unjust. All segregation statutes are unjust because segregation distorts the soul and damages the personality. It gives the segregator a false sense of superiority and the segregated a false sense of inferiority.[†]

The civil rights leader also made certain that those who had referred to his actions as "untimely" knew exactly what had motivated him: "There comes a time when the cup of endurance runs over, and men are no longer willing to be plunged into the abyss of despair. I hope, sirs, you can understand our legitimate and unavoidable impatience."[††] Reverend King's letter would one day be published for the world to read by the American Friends Service Committee, a Quaker organization. It would be reprinted in numerous publications, eventually reaching a million copies in circulation. As a civil rights document, "Letter from Birmingham Jail" would stand as one of the movement's most important and defining pieces of work.

[*] Taylor Branch, *Parting the Waters: America in the King Years, 1954–63.* New York: Simon and Schuster, 1988, p. 737.

[**] Clayborne Carson, et al. *The Eyes on the Prize Civil Rights Reader: Documents, Speeches, and Firsthand Accounts from the Black Freedom Struggle, 1954–1990.* New York: Penguin Books, 1991, p. 155.

[***] Ibid.

[†] Darlene Clark Hine, *The African-American Odyssey.* Upper Saddle River, N.J.: Prentice Hall, 2005, p. 530.

[††] Carson, *Eyes on the Prize*, p. 156.

interstate systems of transportation and public schools, with a threat to cut off federal monies to any state not in compliance. It would also define "literacy" for voters; many Southern states still kept blacks from voting by using literacy tests. The bill proved to civil rights advocates just how much President Kennedy supported the movement, even if he did not always approve of their specific tactics. It was an opportunity for the movement to take its fight out of the streets and into the halls of Congress.

Immediately, leaders of the movement began to organize in favor of the bill. To put pressure on members of Congress to pass it, a group of black organizations, including the SCLC, the NAACP, CORE, the SNCC, and the National Urban League, joined and called for a massive rally to be held in Washington, D.C., later that summer. In August, 250,000 supporters answered the call for a great march on the nation's capital. Among those who spoke was Reverend King, whose "I Have a Dream" speech would be one of the defining moments of the civil rights movement of the 1960s. Before the daylong rally was over, Congress had certainly received the message loud and clear.

White Southerners were not ready to give up their counterefforts against the movement just yet. Within three weeks of the August 28 "March on Washington" the 16th Street Baptist Church in Birmingham, which had been a rallying center for the civil rights movement during the previous five years, was bombed. Four little girls—Addie Mae Collins, Denise McNair, Carole Robertson, and Cynthia Wesley—were inside the church at the time and were killed in the explosion. (Another friend of the girls, young Condoleezza Rice, was not present in the church that day. She grew up to become U.S. secretary of state.) Innocent children had been abused months earlier with fire hoses, attack dogs, and nightsticks. Now, four black girls were dead. Still, Reverend King called for calm and resolution: "The innocent blood of these little girls may well serve as the redemptive force that will bring new light to this dark city. . . . Indeed, this tragic event may cause the white South to come to terms with its conscience."[90]

On August 28, 1963, Martin Luther King Jr. delivered his now legendary "I Have a Dream" speech, which promoted a future in which whites and blacks coexisted peacefully as equals. The speech, which was delivered during the March on Washington, was heard by more than 250,000 civil rights supporters.

Two months later, another killing would have a direct impact on the civil rights movement and the potential for passing the proposed civil rights legislation before Congress.

While President Kennedy was on a visit to Dallas, Texas, Lee Harvey Oswald, a deranged and bitter gunman, shot and killed him. This was the first presidential assassination in more than 60 years. The country immediately began to mourn the president's death. Questions concerning how Kennedy's assissination would affect the civil rights legislation arose in the black community. That issue was addressed shortly after Vice President Lyndon Baines Johnson was sworn in as the new president. Johnson made it clear that he would fight for the bill. He lobbied Congress and twisted arms, promoting the legislation as a tribute to Kennedy's legacy. Although Southern legislators tried to filibuster the bill, it passed and Johnson signed this landmark legislation into law on July 2, 1964.

The Civil Rights Act of 1964 was a significant step forward in the fight for black equality at that juncture of the civil rights movement. No longer could places such as hotels, motels, restaurants, gas stations, theaters, schools, parks, playgrounds, libraries, swimming pools, and similar public and private facilities and grounds be kept segregated. Discrimination by employers based on race, color, religion, national origin, and sex was illegal. To monitor compliance, the act created the Equal Employment Opportunity Commission. The act also had some teeth. Any programs or institutions that received public monies, including schools, could have their federal support denied on the basis of noncompliance.

There was a significant shortcoming to the new act, however, one that had bothered civil rights supporters from the start: It hardly mentioned any assurances to guarantee the vote for the nation's blacks. Some had already begun to take steps on that front, however. President Kennedy had encouraged civil rights leaders to take significant steps on behalf of voter registration in the spring of 1963, and the civil rights movement would now make that its number one goal.

10

Freedom Summer

After President Kennedy's presentation of a new civil rights bill to Congress in the fall of 1963, some elements of the black-led movement for equality were already busy at work on a new campaign, one that sought to change the political role and power of blacks throughout the country. That autumn, CORE and SNCC members launched their drive to register Southern blacks to vote. CORE centered its efforts in Louisiana, South Carolina, and Florida, and SNCC members hit the highways and byways of Alabama and Mississippi.

"GET OUT THE VOTE"

Mississippi had one of the lowest rates of registered black voters—just 1 in 20. With a statewide black population that made up 45 percent of the state's total population, blacks could have controlled politics in many Mississippi counties where they formed the majority. The state was notorious for its high number of random lynchings and attacks on blacks. Life for a black resident of Mississippi during the previous decade had been so difficult and oppressive that more than 300,000 had left the state completely to take up residence elsewhere, usually a Northern city. At the end of the 1950s, the state was home to only 60 black doctors, 5 black lawyers, and a single black dentist. There was little in Mississippi to make life tolerable for its black residents, and few whites went out of their way to support blacks. Few states were as backward and needed change more than Mississippi.

Despite the high level of racism in the state, there had been at least some symbolic successes in Mississippi. In September 1962, James Meredith, a young black man who wanted to break the color barrier at the University of Mississippi at Oxford, won his suit against the university in the U.S. Supreme Court. When the state's governor, Ross Barnett, declared that he would not enforce the court's decision, President Kennedy dispatched 300 federal marshals to Mississippi to do it for him. Rioting had broken out at "Ole Miss"; it involved thousands of white students and others and resulted in hundreds of arrests, injuries for half of the marshals, and the deaths of two individuals. Kennedy was even compelled to federalize Mississippi's National Guard and to use troops to force Meredith's admission to the university. That same summer, Kennedy would face down Alabama governor George Wallace and desegregate the University of Alabama.

The campaign to "get out the vote" in Mississippi began on a limited basis in the fall of 1963 and would not hit its stride until the summer of 1964. The campaign's activities involved volunteers from CORE, the SCLC, the NAACP, and the SNCC, largely working together under a special umbrella organization called the Council of Federated Organizations (COFO). That summer, COFO members requested that Northern white students join them in their voter registration campaign. More than a thousand answered the call. Although the move ran against the concept of blacks empowering one another for the cause of equality, civil rights leaders believed that it would help the campaign receive greater media attention. Those who volunteered were young, the average age 21. Three hundred of the volunteers were women. They came from upper-middle-class families, most of them from New York. Mississippi whites resented them, considering them meddlers, "problem brats, sexually promiscuous, addicted to interracial lovemaking, brainwashed on Communist doctrines."[91]

THREE TRAGIC DEATHS

Tragedy struck the campaign early that summer when, on June 21, two white Northern volunteers—New Yorkers Michael Schwerner and Andrew Goodman, ages 24 and 21, respectively, and James Chaney, a 21-year-old black Mississippi civil rights worker, suddenly disappeared while organizing voter registration. The three young men had last been seen driving to the town of Lawndale to follow up on a report of a black church burning. They had been stopped in their blue Ford station wagon by Cecil Price a local deputy sheriff, arrested on speeding charges, and then released after nightfall. That was the last time they had officially been seen. When Price was informed that they were missing, he expressed little concern: "If they're missing, they're just hid somewhere trying to get a lot of publicity out of it, I figure."[92]

President Kennedy sent FBI agents and federal troops to Mississippi to help in the search through local swamps to find the three missing volunteers. The search continued through the summer. Acts of violence against civil rights volunteers also continued: "Thirty homes and thirty-seven churches were bombed, thirty-five civil rights workers were shot at, eighty people were beaten, six were murdered, and more than one thousand were arrested."[93] Despite these intimidations and the lingering mystery of the three missing workers, "Freedom Summer" volunteers continued their efforts, refusing to be intimidated.

On August 4, after the FBI paid informants inside one of the local Ku Klux Klan chapters (a $30,000 reward served as a powerful incentive) the three missing young men were found buried in a remote earthen dam. They had been left by the sheriff's department on a lonely country road outside Philadelphia, Mississippi, and picked up by three cars full of Klansmen. The two whites were subsequently shot with a .38-caliber handgun. Chaney was beaten with chains and then shot. In December, the FBI finally arrested 21 of those allegedly involved in the killings, including Price, who had stopped the three workers for speeding in the first place. Charges would subsequently be dropped in a Mississippi state court. (Six of the accused would later go to jail when convicted of violating several federal civil rights laws.) Although the courts again disappointed blacks who were seeking justice, the summer's voter registration had been a success, one that would continue to bear fruit in future years.

SELMA

That summer had also witnessed the passage of the Civil Rights Act of 1964, another success for the movement. Civil rights advocates remained disappointed that the act did not include any significant assurances that blacks would be allowed to vote without white-imposed restrictions. Even after the act became law, more than three of every four potential black voters in Alabama were being denied the basic right to cast their ballots. Alabama would become an important state for the voter registration campaign that summer. One of the most important efforts took place in Selma, Alabama. There, veteran civil rights advocate and organizer Amelia Boynton led a battle for black equality that would directly affect the passage of another congressional law: the Voting Rights Act of 1965.

As Boynton, her husband, and local Selma high school teacher Frederick Reese organized voter registration, they met opposition from the local sheriff, James G. Clark Jr. Clark managed to keep the number of registered black voters low—400 out of a potential 15,000—by threatening violence against those who wanted to register. Such defiance was a blatant violation of the U.S. Constitution's Fifteenth Amendment, ratified in 1870, which rendered race discrimination in voting a federal offense. When Reverend King came to Selma early in 1965, he spoke to a crowd of 700 gathered in Brown Chapel African Methodist Episcopal Church. There, he delivered his usual message that endorsed nonviolence. His words ringing in the sanctuary, King assured his listeners that, "We will seek to arouse the federal government by marching by the thousands [to] the place of registration. When we get the right to vote, we will send to the statehouse not men who will stand in the doorways of universities to keep Negroes out, but men who will uphold the cause of justice. Give us the ballot."[94] During the following weeks, as blacks marched to the county courthouse to register, they were met with police nightsticks and arrested. King himself would be arrested in early February. From his jail cell, as he had done while incarcerated in Birmingham, King wrote a letter that was published in the pages of the *New York Times*. In the letter, he claimed, "There are more Negroes in jail with me than there are on the voting rolls."[95]

As in Birmingham, 500 Selma schoolchildren were encouraged to march on the county courthouse after King's arrest. Again, television cameras caught the white response on film: Hundreds of black children were arrested and placed in makeshift "jails" with no toilets. Not long afterward, a civil rights worker was shot in neighboring Perry County by a state police officer. The shooting brought further media attention as television cameras focused on Selma, Alabama.

To protest the shooting, Reverend King, subsequently released from jail on bond, and other leaders of the SCLC

In protest of the shooting of a civil rights worker in Perry County, Alabama, Martin Luther King Jr. organized a large march from Selma to Montgomery on March 7, 1965. Unfortunately, shortly after they left Selma, the 600 civil rights marchers were confronted by police. What resulted came to be known as "Bloody Sunday," during which many marchers were beaten with billy clubs by police and forced to endure tear gas.

called for a large march from Selma to Montgomery, to begin on the morning of Sunday, March 7. King led the march. Behind him followed 600 supporters. They began that Sunday morning by crossing the Edmund Pettus Bridge and then followed Route 80 to Montgomery, Alabama's capital. The march was met with violence at the hands of local police and state troopers, who lobbed tear gas at them, beat them, and trampled several with their horses. The day would be remembered as "Bloody Sunday." Undaunted, King organized another march for two days later.

The march and its organizer soon faced a roadblock. President Johnson, as well as Justice Department officials, asked King to cancel the event. Then, federal Judge Frank M. Johnson, who wanted to hold a hearing on the proposed march before he issued an order for state officials to refrain from interfering with it, issued an injunction. (Judge Johnson usually supported such civil rights actions.) King could either cancel the march or defy a court order. He did not cancel the march, because as he said "we've gone too far now to turn back."[96] Dr. King encouraged his fellow marchers when they gathered in Brown Chapel: "Alabama and our nation have a date with destiny."[97]

"WE SHALL OVERCOME"

On March 9, a crowd of more than 1,500 would-be marchers had gathered at the church. King led his flock to the Pettus Bridge, where Alabama State troopers were gathered, blocking their way as they had done two days earlier. The state police major, John Cloud, instructed the marchers as they approached: "You are ordered to stop. Stand where you are. This march will not continue."[98] For the moment, the protesters did stop, standing arm in arm and swaying from side to side as they sang the movement's anthem, "We Shall Overcome." Then, Reverend King asked fellow minister and civil rights leader Ralph Abernathy to deliver a prayer. Once Abernathy finished his benediction, King surprised everyone by taking up the march in the opposite direction, back toward the church. The protesters were stunned. What was King doing?

King simply gave up the march. When asked later why he decided to abandon the march he had considered part of Alabama's rendezvous with destiny, he explained that he had agreed to lead the march only until it appeared that police violence would take place. With the threat of violence in front of them, King said, he had proven his point: that state officials would use every tactic and force at their disposal to stop the progress of the civil rights movement and that violence would continue even after the march was halted. That evening, King went to dinner with two white ministers. As they exited the restaurant, the ministers were attacked. One of them suffered wounds to his head after being beaten with a club and died two days later.

In the days after the aborted second march at Selma, events moved forward. President Johnson assured civil rights leaders that Congress would pass the new civil rights legislation. Many of the marchers remained in and around the grounds of Brown Chapel, waiting to see what King might ask of them. On March 12, Reverend King went on to Montgomery to attend the hearing held by Judge Johnson. Selma officials, including Sheriff Clark, were also present. Clark asked that King be held in contempt of court. The judge refused but did not issue a ruling that day. Meanwhile in Washington, President Johnson met with Alabama governor George Wallace, who had flown to the White House on a powder-blue state airplane adorned with a Confederate flag. The president tried to get Wallace to comply with the march, and Wallace seemed to give the president some hope that he might cooperate.

Two days later, on March 15, President Johnson appeared on national television to talk to the American people about the events that had been taking place in Selma. He referred to them as "an American tragedy." He likened those involved in the marches and demonstrations to symbols of the American spirit. "Their cause must be our cause, too," the president said. At the end of his address, Johnson used the movement's most popular phrase: "We shall overcome."[99] That evening, King and other leaders of the movement, along with hundreds of supporters, met at Brown Chapel. King addressed the crowd, telling them that he was "not satisfied as long as the Negro sees life as a long and empty corridor with a 'No Exit' sign at the end."[100] The anxious crowd was ready to take up the march again, but King still wanted to postpone it until the court order was issued. Relief of the impasse came later that evening, when one of the movement's key leaders, Andrew Young, came to the church and gave King the news: Judge Johnson had given the march from Selma to Montgomery the green light.

THE ROAD TO MONTGOMERY

Despite the court order and the recent pressure exerted on him by President Johnson, Governor Wallace remained uncooperative. He would not provide state police to protect the marchers, claiming that Alabama could not cover the cost financially. President Johnson then made a countermove and federalized the Alabama National Guard, deploying 1,800 troops to guard the demonstrators on the road to Montgomery. To assist them, the president also sent 2,000 regular army troops and 100 each of FBI agents and federal marshals. Literally, a national army was being delivered to Alabama to protect an army of civil rights demonstrators. The march was set for Sunday, March 21.

It would be larger than any previous civil rights march during the King-led years of the movement. Four thousand supporters, both black and white, gathered once more at Brown Chapel to take up their 50-mile march to Montgomery. Many had never engaged in a civil rights march before. Among the new faces was Ralph Bunche, a black political scientist who had helped draft the United Nations Charter in the 1940s and had won the Nobel Peace Prize for mediating a truce between Israel and Egypt, Jordan, Lebanon, and Syria after the conclusion of the Arab-Israeli War in 1948. Marchers included Jewish leaders, as well as Catholic priests and nuns. The scope and diversity of the civil rights movement had certainly expanded over the years since the 1950s. As the marchers moved along Route 80 toward Montgomery, they were greeted with a long and constant stream of detractors and white segregationists who shouted, "Yankee trash go home." Unlike the earlier march from Selma, though, there was no violence. The diligent efforts of the federal forces sent to protect the marchers included checking sites off the road for rifle-toting would-be assassins.

All along the route, new marchers joined the civil rights caravan. Soon, the original 4,000 doubled and then doubled again. Before the march was completed, more than 25,000 people, blacks and whites, moved together in a massive march that symbolized the best that the civil rights movement had to offer: nonviolent protest carried out in the spirit of brotherly love and harmonious conviction to right the wrongs of the past and present. As the line of supporters marched along, they were sometimes inspired by Leroy Moton, a 15-year-old black youth who carried the U.S. flag and often broke out singing the national anthem. Marchers would join him, the words to the "Star-Spangled Banner" drifting down the line.

The march lasted five days. Nights were spent on the road: Marchers pitched tents and a revolving fleet of cars delivered food to the weary demonstrators. As the marchers approached the outskirts of Montgomery, word circulated of a plot to kill Reverend King. Undaunted by the threat, King would not leave the march to protect his life. To help protect King and possibly confuse a would-be assassin, Andrew Young had every black man in the march who was approximately King's height and wearing a dark blue suit (such a suit was King's standard blue "preacher" suit) move to the front of the line and march in front of Dr. King. Young did not fully explain why he made such an odd request to those who were possibly serving as a human shield to the civil rights leader.

As the protesters engaged in their symbolic march, the proposed civil rights bill was being presented to Congress. Already, the march on Montgomery was having an impact on its possible passage. As the House Judiciary Committee considered the bill, one congressman reminded his colleagues, "Recent events in Alabama, involving murder, savage brutality, and violence by local police, state troopers, and posses, have so aroused the nation as to make action by this Congress necessary and speedy."[101]

On Thursday, March 25, the marchers passed Montgomery's Dexter Avenue Baptist Church, the church where Dr. King had rallied supporters for the Montgomery bus boycott a decade earlier. On they marched to the state capitol, with television cameras rolling, catching the details of the historic march with live coverage. Once they arrived at the capitol, King strode up the steps, along with a pantheon of civil rights organizers and leaders: Reverend Abernathy; Roy Wilkins of the NAACP; A. Philip Randolph, who had led his first civil rights rally in Washington, D.C., in 1941; John Lewis of the SNCC; and Whitney Young of the National Urban League. With them was one of the great symbols of the movement: Rosa Parks, who had served as the catalyst for the Montgomery bus boycott. It was a crowning moment for the movement, one rife with dignity and hope for the future.

ON THE CAPITOL STEPS

With the Confederate flag flying over the state house and Governor Wallace peeking from behind the venetian blinds of his office window, Reverend King addressed the triumphant crowd. He knew that everyone was tired but proud of their accomplishment. He assured them that

On March 25, 1965, approximately 25,000 civil rights activists gathered in front of the Alabama state capitol in Montgomery to conclude the Selma-to-Montgomery march. Some of the individuals who took part in the march are pictured here at the state capitol, where they are protesting Alabama's voter registration laws.

their actions were being noted and that their voices were being heard: "I stand before you this afternoon with the conviction that segregation is on its deathbed in Alabama and the only thing uncertain about it is how costly the segregationists and Wallace will make the funeral."[102] The civil rights bill would be passed, he told them, and, when it was, blacks would become equal in the eyes of the law and be able to live in a "society at peace with itself, a society that can live with its conscience."[103] King knew that the fight for civil rights would not end with the passage of the important bill before Congress and that the campaign would continue by registering as many blacks as possible to vote. "The road ahead is not altogether a smooth one," he reminded his supporters. "We are still in for a season of suffering."[104]

After King's speech, eight civil rights advocates strode up the steps of the capitol and past a phalanx of state troopers and city officials carrying riot guns with bayonets mounted. They explained that they were there to see Governor Wallace to present him with a petition that called for him to take the responsibility to eliminate all the state restrictions to black voter registration. Officials told them that the governor was not available and then agreed to give the petition to Wallace themselves. The march was complete. Thousands of blacks, along with white supporters, had walked more than 50 miles from Selma to Montgomery and made their petition known. They had done so without carrying out any violence in the name of the important cause.

During the next two months, the Voting Rights Act gained greater support, in part because of the violence that Southern whites had perpetrated against the Selma marchers. Debate bogged the bill down for a time over the issue of banning poll taxes, which were still in place in four Southern states in order to deny blacks their right to vote. To help pave the way for ridding the nation of poll taxes, President Johnson instructed the Justice Department to file suits against those four states—Alabama, Mississippi, Texas, and Virginia—for their long-standing use of the poll tax. On May 26, the bill passed through the Senate with a vote of 77 to 19. The bill was further delayed in the House, which finally passed the proposed legislation on July 9.

A month later, on August 6, 1965, President Johnson hosted a formal signing ceremony in the President's Room, just off the U.S. Capitol's rotunda. In that same room, Abraham Lincoln had signed the Emancipation Proclamation 103 years earlier. Flanking the president as he placed his name on the new law were several civil rights leaders, including Martin Luther King Jr. and Rosa Parks. "[This act] is one of the most monumental laws in the entire history of American freedom," said Johnson. "The vote is the most powerful instrument ever devised by man for breaking down injustice and destroying the terrible walls which imprison men because they are different from other men."[105] It was a sublime moment for the civil rights movement.

A MAJOR VICTORY FOR THE MOVEMENT

With the passage of the Voting Rights Act of 1965, the civil rights movement had accomplished one of its most significant successes. It would not mark the end of segregation in the United States, raise the standard of living for many blacks, or address unemployment, but it was a great symbol of the movement. In the vote, blacks found yet another way to express their political wants and needs. The act began to have other almost immediate and positive results. As blacks cast their ballots throughout the country, they were able to elect many of their own race to public offices that ranged from mayor to legislator to congressional representative. For the first time since the days after the Civil War, blacks were electing blacks to political office. In Alabama, James Clark failed to win his next election for sheriff because of the ballots cast by 9,000 black voters.

During the decades after the passage of this singularly significant voting rights law, blacks continued to make inroads. That same year, President Johnson chose Thurgood Marshall, the great civil rights lawyer and advocate in the *Brown v. Board of Education of Topeka* case, as his solicitor general. In 1967, Johnson nominated Marshall for a seat on the U.S. Supreme Court; Marshall was the first black man chosen for the highest court in the land. Johnson would also appoint the first black to hold a cabinet position. In the

On June 13, 1967, Thurgood Marshall became the first African-American Supreme Court justice when he was appointed to that post by President Lyndon B. Johnson. During the next 24 years, Marshall served on the court where he advocated the constitutional protection of individual rights.

1970s, President Jimmy Carter appointed Andrew Young, Martin Luther King Jr.'s right-hand man in the NAACP in Atlanta, as ambassador to the United Nations. Young would go on to become Atlanta's first black mayor. He would not

THE ASSASSINATION OF MARTIN LUTHER KING

The civil rights movement, under a decade of leadership by Reverend Martin Luther King Jr., witnessed the successful passage of the Civil Rights Act of 1965. However, the days of King's influence were drawing to a close. Within less than three years, King was assassinated. That period would prove to be a frustrating time of redefinition of the movement and for himself as the movement's touchstone and chief motivator.

After 1965, King was increasingly criticized, not only by whites who considered him a radical black leader, but from blacks who thought that King had served his purpose but was keeping the movement from becoming as militant as they thought it should be. During 1965 and 1966, King shifted his campaign out of the South and into the North, where he hoped to "demonstrate the national range of the civil rights movement."[*] He was certain that he would find support in Northern cities from both whites and blacks. He found neither to the extent he expected.

When he organized marches in Chicago, Mayor Richard Daley instructed his police force to allow King to demonstrate, wanting no violence. This move countered King's strategy, which was to march to provoke confrontation. In black neighborhoods, he found himself sometimes reviled by black militants who thought that he was too soft on the white establishment.

King's Northern urban marches did drive home an important set of points for the civil rights leader. Racial discrimination was a national problem, and it was linked to the nation's economic system. By 1967, Reverend King began to refocus his struggle toward poverty and economic inequality. His reasoning was clear: "What good is it to be

be alone. By the mid-1980s, more than 250 American cities were being served by black mayors.

Much of the change between the races in the United States that has come during the past 40 years has taken place allowed to sit in a restaurant if you can't afford a hamburger?"** That fall, he launched his nonviolent "Poor People's Campaign." The centerpiece of the campaign was a march on Washington in the spring of 1968 by tens of thousands of poor Americans, black and white alike. King asked federal leaders to guarantee a minimum income for all Americans. The campaign would never gain much traction. When King began to criticize President Johnson about his Vietnam War policies, Johnson turned against King, as did other civil rights leaders who were Johnson supporters.

That spring would be Reverend King's last. Following a new strategy to connect with major labor issues, King traveled to Memphis to support an all-black labor union of sanitation workers, which was on strike. During the final weeks of March and early April, King called for the city to settle with the 1,300 striking sanitation workers. Then, on April 4, King was gunned down while standing on the balcony of the Lorraine Motel, shot by a rifle-toting white assassin named James Earl Ray. King's murder sparked a period of national mourning and a backlash of violence in America's black communities. During the week after his death, riots broke out in 125 U.S. cities, resulting in the deaths of 46 people, along with 35,000 injuries and 20,000 arrests.

King's death was not in vain. Although he had lost much of his support in Congress and with President Johnson, the Civil Rights Act of 1968 was passed just days after his assassination. The act placed a federal ban on discrimination in housing.

---

* Darlene Clark Hine, *The African-American Odyssey.* Upper Saddle River, N.J.: Prentice Hall, 2005, p. 557.
** Ibid.

because of the efforts made by those who supported the civil rights movement for the past 50 or 60 years. Those who led the charge in the 1950s and 1960s did not start the movement. Important civil rights leaders such as Martin Luther King Jr.,

Ralph Abernathy, Andrew Young, Rosa Parks, and others had merely continued the movement, building on the work carried out by those advocates who proceeded them. The wonderful decade between the Supreme Court's *Brown* decisions in 1954–1955 through the passage of the Voting Rights Act of 1965, was one of momentous achievement, filled with anguish and hope, tears and conviction, struggle and success. Violence against the movement, however, would not end even in later years. Reverend King was assassinated by James Earl Ray in the spring of 1968. Robert Kennedy, who had reluctantly helped King and others during the Freedom Rides, was also killed by an assassin just two months after King's death. With each loss among the ranks of those who fought for their equal rights, 100 more rose up to take their places. Their sacrifices would be rewarded as they struggled on behalf of countless brothers and sisters they did not know. The actions taken by tens of thousands had not changed the United States merely for their benefit; they had risked everything so that millions might enjoy, in words found in Abraham Lincoln's Gettysburg Address, a new birth of freedom.

CHRONOLOGY

1863   President Lincoln's Emancipation Proclamation begins the liberation of black slaves in the United States.

1865   The U.S. Congress passes the Thirteenth Amendment to the Constitution, freeing all slaves in the United States; the states ratify the amendment before year's end.

1865–1866   Southern states pass Black Codes, limiting the rights of blacks and denying them equality.

1866   Congress passes the Civil Rights Act of 1866, which declares that anyone born in the United States is a citizen and that their rights are guaranteed by law.

1868   States ratify the Fourteenth Amendment, granting citizenship to all Americans, including former slaves.

1869   Congress passes the Fifteenth Amendment, granting full rights, including the right to vote, to black men, even former slaves.

1871   Georgia begins to require a poll tax before anyone can vote; the law is intended to limit the number of black voters.

1875   Congress passes the Civil Rights Act of 1875, which is designed to eliminate as many loopholes as possible that formerly denied blacks equal rights.

1877   Reconstruction ends throughout the South, along with the federal protections it had provided blacks, including former slaves.

1880s–1890s Many laws are passed throughout the South to require segregation of the black and white races; such laws are known as "Jim Crow" laws.

1881 Tennessee passes the first "separate but equal" law, segregating railroad cars in the state.

1883 The U.S. Supreme Court declares the Civil Rights Act of 1875 to be unconstitutional, stating that it violates the Fourteenth Amendment.

1889–1932 Approximately 3,750 people are lynched in the United States, most of them in the South and the vast majority of them black.

1895 South Carolina adopts an "understanding clause" as a requirement to vote; the law

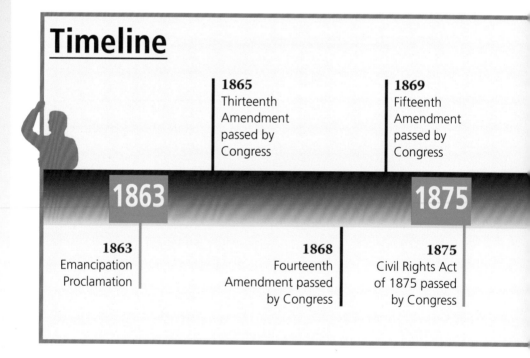

Timeline

1865
Thirteenth Amendment passed by Congress

1869
Fifteenth Amendment passed by Congress

1863

1875

1863
Emancipation Proclamation

1868
Fourteenth Amendment passed by Congress

1875
Civil Rights Act of 1875 passed by Congress

intends to keep blacks from voting by declaring them illiterate.

1896 The U.S. Supreme Court decision *Plessy v. Ferguson* establishes "separate but equal" as law throughout the United States.

1909 The NAACP is established as an early-twentieth-century civil rights organization.

1915 NAACP attorneys win *Guinn v. United States*, which overturns a black voting restriction called a "grandfather clause" in Oklahoma.

1917 Lawyers for the NAACP win *Buchanan v. Warley*, a Kentucky case that grants blacks the right to live in white-majority neighborhoods.

1920 NAACP membership mushrooms from 9,000 in 1916 to nearly 100,000 in this year.

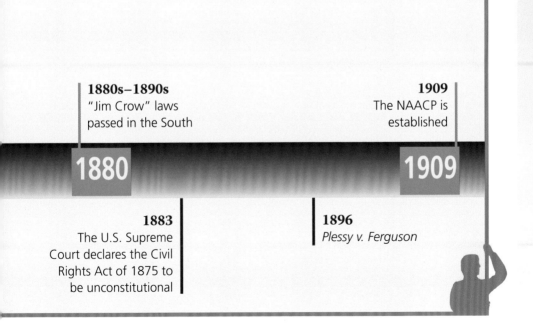

1880s–1890s
"Jim Crow" laws
passed in the South

1909
The NAACP is
established

1880

1909

1883
The U.S. Supreme
Court declares the Civil
Rights Act of 1875 to
be unconstitutional

1896
Plessy v. Ferguson

1920s   The NAACP battles against lynching, calling
                   for antilynching federal legislation.

1930s   Blacks in the United States struggle through the
                   Great Depression with few federal laws in place
                   to provide them jobs.

1936   NAACP attorney Charles Houston wins
                   Pearson v. Murray, a case that strikes down
                   the University of Maryland's admissions policy,
                   under which only white students were accepted.

1939   NAACP attorneys win *Lane v. Wilson*, which
                   strikes down an Oklahoma law that restricted
                   black voting.

January 1941   A. Philip Randolph, black president of the
                   Brotherhood of Sleeping Car Porters, leads a
                   massive rally and march on Washington, D.C.,
                   calling for equal employment opportunities for

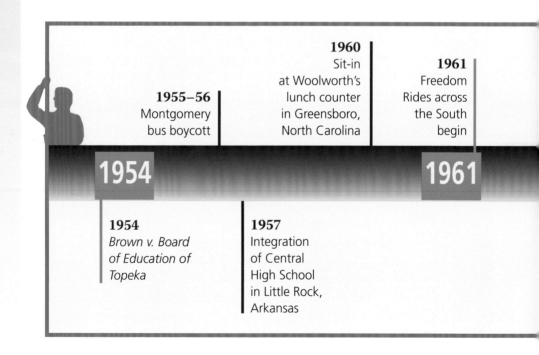

1960
Sit-in
at Woolworth's
lunch counter
in Greensboro,
North Carolina

1961
Freedom
Rides across
the South
begin

1955–56
Montgomery
bus boycott

1954

1961

1954
*Brown v. Board
of Education of
Topeka*

1957
Integration
of Central
High School
in Little Rock,
Arkansas

blacks and an end to segregation in the U.S. military.

June 1941   President Franklin Roosevelt issues Executive Order 8802, which calls for an end to discrimination in the employment of workers in the defense industry and the government.

1941–1945   American blacks serve in a segregated U.S. military during World War II.

1944   NAACP attorney Thurgood Marshall successfully argues *Smith v. Allwright*, which strikes down a Texas law that denied blacks the vote in primary elections.

1946   Marshall wins the Supreme Court case *Morgan v. Virginia*, which strikes down a Virginia law that denied blacks the right to sit in the seats of their choice on an interstate bus.

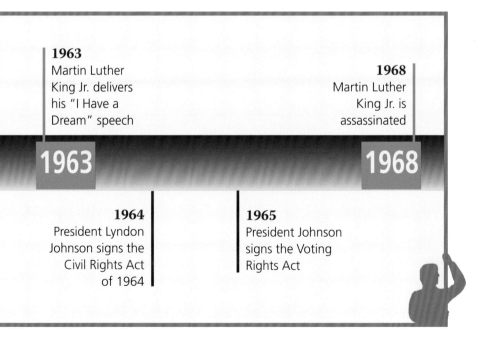

1963
Martin Luther King Jr. delivers his "I Have a Dream" speech

1968
Martin Luther King Jr. is assassinated

1963

1968

1964
President Lyndon Johnson signs the Civil Rights Act of 1964

1965
President Johnson signs the Voting Rights Act

1950	Marshall wins two Supreme Court cases, *Sweatt v. Painter* and *McLaurin v. Oklahoma State Regents for Higher Education*; both cases are concerned with blacks being denied entry to professional schools.
1954	Thurgood Marshall successfully argues another landmark case before the Supreme Court; *Brown v. Board of Education of Topeka* strikes a death blow against the concept of "separate but equal."
December 1955	Chicago youth Emmett Till is lynched in Mississippi for saying "Bye, baby" to the wife of a white storeowner; the circumstances of his death shock many Americans; that same month, blacks organize the Montgomery (Alabama) bus boycott after Rosa Parks is arrested for refusing to surrender her bus seat to a white person.
December 1956	The Montgomery bus boycott finally ends after 381 days; the boycott launches the national career of Reverend Martin Luther King Jr., America's most prominent civil rights leader.
February 1957	The Southern Christian Leadership Conference (SCLC) is organized in New Orleans by black civil rights organizers; Martin Luther King Jr. is selected as the organization's first president.
August 1957	Congress passes the Civil Rights Act of 1957.
September 1957	President Dwight Eisenhower sends federal troops to aid in the integration of Central High School in Little Rock, Arkansas.
1958	Black civil rights leaders in Nashville begin to offer workshops to train protesters in the tactic of passive resistance.

February 1960	Four students from North Carolina A&T College engage in a sit-in at the Woolworth's lunch counter in Greensboro, North Carolina.
April 1960	The Student Nonviolent Coordinating Committee (SNCC) is organized at Shaw University in Raleigh, North Carolina.
May 1961	Freedom Rides across the South, organized by the Congress of Racial Equality (CORE), begin.
September 1961	The Interstate Commerce Commission (ICC) issues a ruling that prohibits segregation in interstate buses and facilities, such as bus stations.
April 1963	A series of civil rights protests is launched in Birmingham, Alabama; they are organized by the Alabama Christian Movement for Human Rights (ACMHR) and the SCLC.
June 1963	Executive secretary of the Mississippi NAACP Medgar Evers is gunned down in his driveway.
August 1963	Martin Luther King Jr. delivers his "I Have a Dream" speech in Washington, D.C., during a massive march on the nation's capital.
September 1963	Four young black girls are killed when a bomb destroys the 16th Street Baptist Church in Birmingham.
July 1964	President Lyndon Johnson signs the Civil Rights Act of 1964.
August 1964	Three civil rights workers—Andrew Goodman, Michael Schwerner, and James Chaney—are murdered in Mississippi while working to register the state's black voters.
January 1965	Reverend King speaks at Brown Chapel in Selma, Alabama.

March 1965   King leads the Selma-to-Montgomery march, which reaches the steps of the Alabama state house.

August 1965   President Johnson signs the Voting Rights Act.

January 1966   King launches the Chicago movement, which ends in relative failure.

March 1968   King launches the SCLC's Poor People's Campaign.

April 1968   Martin Luther King Jr. is assassinated in Memphis, Tennessee.

NOTES

CHAPTER 1

1. Juan Williams, *Eyes on the Prize: America's Civil Rights Years, 1954–1965* (New York: Penguin Books, 2002), 190.
2. Ibid., 195.
3. Tim McNeese and Michael S. Mountjoy, *History in the Making: Sources and Essays of America's Past*, vol. 2 (New York: American Heritage, 1994), 328.

CHAPTER 2

4. Darlene Clark Hine, *The African-American Odyssey* (Upper Saddle River, N.J.: Prentice Hall, 2005), 277.
5. Tim McNeese, *The U.S. Constitution* (St. Louis, Mo.: Milliken, 2001), 92.
6. Hine, *African-American Odyssey*, 296.
7. Ibid., 263.
8. Ibid., 276.
9. Ibid., 279.
10. Ibid., 298.

CHAPTER 3

11. James Tackach, *Brown v. Board of Education* (San Diego, Calif.: Lucent Books, 1998), 17.
12. Harvey Fireside and Sarah Betsy Fuller, *Brown v. Board of Education: Equal School for All* (Hillside, N.J.: Enslow, 1994), 23.
13. Edward L. Ayers, *The Promise of the New South: Life After Reconstruction* (New York: Oxford University Press, 1992), 136.
14. Ibid.
15. Hine, *African-American Odyssey*, 316.
16. Ayers, *Promise of the New South*, 136.
17. David Levering Lewis, *W. E. B. Du Bois: Biography of a Race, 1868–1919* (New York: Henry Holt, 1993), 313.
18. Hine, *African-American Odyssey*, 429.
19. Ibid., 483.
20. Ibid, 484.
21. Ibid., 485.
22. Ibid., 489.
23. Ibid., 489–490.
24. Ibid., 492.
25. Ibid.
26. Ibid., 493.

CHAPTER 4

27. Tim McNeese, *Brown v. Board of Education: Integrating America's Schools* (New York: Chelsea House, 2007), 47.
28. Ibid., 67.
29. Robert J. Cottroll, Raymond T. Diamond, and Leland B.

Ware, *Brown v. Board of Education: Caste, Culture, and the Constitution* (Lawrence: University of Kansas Press, 2003), 55.

30. Williams, *Eyes on the Prize*, 60.
31. Ibid., 61.
32. Ibid., 62
33. Ibid., 63.
34. Ibid.
35. Ibid., 66.
36. Taylor Branch, *Parting the Waters: America in the King Years, 1954–63* (New York: Simon and Schuster, 1988), 128.
37. Clayborne Carson, et al. *The Eyes on the Prize Civil Rights Reader: Documents, Speeches, and Firsthand Accounts from the Black Freedom Struggle, 1954–1990* (New York: Penguin Books, 1991), 46.
38. Branch, *Parting the Waters*, 129.

CHAPTER 5

39. Williams, *Eyes on the Prize*, 69.
40. Ibid., 72.
41. Ibid.
42. Ibid., 73.
43. Ibid., 74.
44. Branch, *Parting the Waters*, 136.
45. Williams, *Eyes on the Prize*, 74.
46. Ibid.
47. Hine, *African-American Odyssey*, 519.
48. Williams, *Eyes on the Prize*, 76.
49. Ibid., 77.
50. Ibid.

CHAPTER 6

51. Ibid., 79.
52. Hine, *African-American Odyssey*, 520.
53. Ibid., 521.
54. Williams, *Eyes on the Prize*, 92.
55. Branch, *Parting the Waters*, 224.
56. Ibid.
57. Williams, *Eyes on the Prize*, 107.
58. Ibid.
59. Ibid., 110.
60. Ibid.

CHAPTER 7

61. Hine, *African-American Odyssey*, 525.
62. Ibid., 527.
63. David Halberstam, *The Children* (New York: Random House, 1998), 93.
64. Arthur I. Waskow, *From Race Riot to Sit-In, 1919 and the 1960s* (Garden City, New York: Doubleday, 1966), 227.
65. Andrew Young, *An Easy Burden: The Civil Rights Movement and the Transformation of America* (New York: HarperCollins, 1996), 125.
66. Hine, *African-American Odyssey,* 524.
67. Ibid.

CHAPTER 8

68. Henry Hampton and Steve Fayer, *Voices of Freedom: An Oral History of the Civil Rights Movement from the 1950s through the 1980s* (New York: Bantam Books, 1990), 75.
69. Williams, *Eyes on the Prize,* 148.
70. Ibid.
71. Branch, *Parting the Waters,* 443.
72. Williams, *Eyes on the Prize,* 152.
73. Ibid.
74. Ibid., 153.
75. Branch, *Parting the Waters,* 443.
76. Williams, *Eyes on the Prize,* 153.
77. Ibid.
78. Ibid., 155.
79. Branch, *Parting the Waters,* 453.
80. Ibid., 460.
81. Williams, *Eyes on the Prize,* 157.
82. Ibid., 158–159.
83. Ibid., 159.
84. Ibid., 160.

CHAPTER 9

85. Hine, *African-American Odyssey,* 529.
86. Ibid.
87. Williams, *Eyes on the Prize,* 181.
88. Branch, *Parting the Waters,* 759.
89. Ibid., 760.
90. Hine, *African-American Odyssey,* 531.

CHAPTER 10

91. Jack Mendelsohn, *The Martyrs: Sixteen Who Gave Their Lives for Racial Justice* (New York: Harper & Row, 1966), 125.
92. Williams, *Eyes on the Prize,* 213.
93. Hine, *African-American Odyssey,* 533.
94. Williams, *Eyes on the Prize,* 258.
95. Carson et al., *Eyes on the Prize,* 212.
96. Williams, *Eyes on the Prize,* 274.
97. Ibid.
98. Ibid.
99. Ibid., 278.
100. Ibid., 279.
101. Ibid., 282.
102. Carson, et al., *Eyes on the Prize,* 224.
103. Williams, *Eyes on the Prize,* 283.
104. Carson, et al., *Eyes on the Prize,* 226–227.
105. Williams, *Eyes on the Prize,* 285.

BIBLIOGRAPHY

Ayers, Edward L. *The Promise of the New South: Life After Reconstruction.* New York: Oxford University Press, 1992.

Branch, Taylor. *Parting the Waters: America in the King Years, 1954–63.* New York: Simon and Schuster, 1988.

Carson, Clayborne, David J. Garrow, Gerald Gill, Vincent Harding, and Darlene Clark Hine, eds. *The Eyes on the Prize Civil Rights Reader: Documents, Speeches, and Firsthand Accounts from the Black Freedom Struggle, 1954–1990.* New York: Penguin Books, 1991.

Cottroll, Robert J., Raymond T. Diamond, and Leland B. Ware. *Brown v. Board of Education: Caste, Culture, and the Constitution.* Lawrence: University of Kansas Press, 2003.

Crawford, Vicki L., Jacqueline Anne Rouse, and Barbara Woods, eds. *Women in the Civil Rights Movement: Trailblazers and Torchbearers, 1941–1965.* Bloomington: Indiana University Press, 1993.

Fireside, Harvey, and Sarah Betsy Fuller. *Brown v. Board of Education: Equal School for All.* Hillside, N.J.: Enslow, 1994.

Halberstam, David. *The Children.* New York: Random House, 1998.

Hampton, Henry, and Steve Fayer. *Voices of Freedom: An Oral History of the Civil Rights Movement from the 1950s through the 1980s.* New York: Bantam Books, 1990.

Hine, Darlene Clark. *The African-American Odyssey.* Upper Saddle River, N.J.: Prentice Hall, 2005.

King, Martin Luther, Jr. *Why We Can't Wait.* New York: Harper & Row, 1964.

Lasky, Victor. *Robert F. Kennedy: The Myth and the Man.* New York: Trident Press, 1968.

Lewis, David Levering. *W. E. B. Du Bois: Biography of a Race, 1868–1919.* New York: Henry Holt and Company, 1993.

McNeese, Tim. *Brown v. Board of Education: Integrating America's Schools.* New York: Chelsea House, 2007.

———. *The U.S. Constitution.* St. Louis, Mo.: Milliken, 2001.

McNeese, Tim, and Michael S. Mountjoy. *History in the Making: Sources and Essays of America's Past,* vol. 2. New York: American Heritage, 1994.

Mendelsohn, Jack. *The Martyrs: Sixteen Who Gave Their Lives for Racial Justice.* New York: Harper & Row, 1966.

Tackach, James. *Brown v. Board of Education.* San Diego, Calif.: Lucent Books, 1998.

Waskow, Arthur I. *From Race Riot to Sit-In, 1919 and the 1960s.* Garden City, New York.: Doubleday, 1966.

Williams, Juan. *Eyes on the Prize: America's Civil Rights Years, 1954–1965.* New York: Penguin Books, 2002.

Young, Andrew. *An Easy Burden: The Civil Rights Movement and the Transformation of America.* New York: HarperCollins, 1996.

FURTHER READING

Archer, Jules. *They Had a Dream: The Civil Rights Struggle from Frederick Douglass to Marcus Garvey to Martin Luther King, Jr. and Malcolm X.* New York: Penguin Young Readers Group, 1996.

Beals, Melba Pattillo. *Warriors Don't Cry: A Searing Memoir of the Battle to Integrate Little Rock's Central High.* New York: Simon & Schuster, 1997.

Engelbert, Phillis. *American Civil Rights: Almanac.* San Diego, Calif.: Thomson Gale, 1999.

George, Linda, and Charles George. *Civil Rights Marches.* Danbury, Conn.: Scholastic Library, 2000.

Hardy, Sheila. *Extraordinary People of the Civil Rights Movement.* Danbury, Conn.: Scholastic Library, 2006.

Kudlinski, Kathleen, and Meryl Henderson. *Rosa Parks.* New York: Simon & Schuster, 2001.

Landau, Elaine. *Civil Rights Movement in America.* Danbury, Conn.: Children's Press, 2003.

McWhorter, Diane, and Fred Shuttlesworth. *A Dream of Freedom.* New York: Scholastic, 2004.

Medearis, Angela Shelf. *Dare to Dream: Coretta Scott King and the Civil Rights Movement.* New York: Penguin Young Readers Group, 1998.

Miller, Calvin Craig. *No Easy Answers: Bayard Rustin and the Civil Rights Movement.* Greensboro, N.C.: Morgan Reynolds, 2005.

Miller, Jake. *Brown vs. Board of Education of Topeka: Challenging School Segregation in the Supreme Court.* New York: Rosen, 2004.

Morrison, Toni. *Remember: The Journey to School Integration.* New York: Houghton Mifflin, 2004.

Murcia, Rebecca Thatcher. *Civil Rights Movement.* Hockessin, Del.: Mitchell Lane, 2005.

Rappaport, Doreen. *Nobody Gonna Turn Me 'Round: Stories and Songs of the Civil Rights Movement.* Cambridge, Mass.: Candlewick Press, 2006.

Ritchie, Nigel, and R. G. Grant. *The Civil Rights Movement.* New York: Barron's Educational Series, 2003.

Sirimarco, Elizabeth. *American Voices from the Civil Rights Movement.* Tarrytown, New York: Marshall Cavendish, 2004.

WEB SITES

Black History
www.africanaonline.com/civil_rights.htm

Civil Rights Movement Veterans
www.crmvet.org

We Shall Overcome:
Historic Places of the Civil Rights Movement
www.cr.nps.gov/nr/travel/civilrights

Dr. Martin Luther King Jr.
www.drmartinlutherkingjr.com

Rosa Parks: The Woman Who Changed a Nation
www.grandtimes.com/rosa.html

The Montgomery Bus Boycott
www.montgomeryboycott.com

Voices of Civil Rights:
Ordinary People, Extraordinary Stories
www.voicesofcivilrights.org

PICTURE CREDITS

INDEX

151

ABOUT THE AUTHOR

TIM McNEESE is associate professor of history at York College in York, Nebraska, where he is in his sixteenth year of college instruction. Professor McNeese earned an associate of arts degree from York College, a bachelor of arts in history and political science from Harding University, and a master of arts in history from Missouri State University. A prolific author of books for elementary, middle, and high school and college readers, McNeese has published more than 90 books and educational materials during the past 20 years, on everything from Picasso to landmark Supreme Court decisions. His writing has earned him a citation in the library reference work *Contemporary Authors*. In 2006, McNeese appeared on the History Channel program *Risk Takers/History Makers: John Wesley Powell and the Grand Canyon*. He was a faculty member at the 2006 Tony Hillerman Writers Conference in Albuquerque, New Mexico, where he presented on the topic of American Indians of the Southwest. Professor McNeese was a contributor to the 2007 *World Book Encyclopedia*.